# The Lost Gospel
*of* Mary

# The Lost Gospel
## of Mary

*The Mother of Jesus in Three Ancient Texts*

## Frederica Mathewes-Green

PARACLETE PRESS
BREWSTER, MASSACHUSETTS

*The Lost Gospel of Mary: The Mother of Jesus in Three Ancient Texts*

2007 First Printing

Copyright © 2007 by Frederica Mathewes-Green

ISBN 13: 978-1-55725-536-5

**Library of Congress Cataloging-in-Publication Data**
The lost Gospel of Mary : the Mother of Jesus in three ancient texts / [compiled by] Frederica Mathewes-Green.
   p. cm.
   ISBN 978-1-55725-536-5
   1. Mary, Blessed Virgin, Saint. I. Mathewes-Green, Frederica.
II. Romanus, Melodus, Saint, 6th cent. Akathist salutations to the Virgin. English. III. Protevangelium Jacobi. English. IV. Sub tuum praesidium. English.
   BT603.L67 2007
   232.91—dc22                                      2006100852

10 9 8 7 6 5 4 3 2 1

Published by Paraclete Press
Brewster, Massachusetts
www.paracletepress.com

Printed in the United States of America

DEDICATED TO THE MEMORY OF

FR. GEORGE CALCIU,

*my spiritual father,*

*who fell asleep in the Lord on November 21, 2006,*

*the Feast of the Presentation of the Theotokos*

*Her hands steadied the first steps
of him who steadied the earth to walk upon;
her lips helped the Word of God
to form his first human words.*

—ST. JOHN OF DAMASCUS (AD 676–780)

# CONTENTS

# The Beloved
# Virgin Mary

*Who was she?*

IT IS HARD TO SEE MARY CLEARLY, beneath the conflicting identities she has borne over the centuries. To one era she is the flower of femininity, and to another the champion of feminism; in one age she is the paragon of obedience, and in another the advocate of liberation. Some enthusiasts have been tempted to pile her status so high that it rivals that of her Son. Others, aware that excessive adulation can be dangerous, do their best to ignore her entirely.

Behind all that there is a woman nursing a baby. The child in her arms looks into her eyes. Years later he will look at her from the cross, through a haze of blood and sweat. We do not know, could not comprehend, what went through his mind during those hours of cosmic warfare. But from a moment in the St. John's account of the Crucifixion we know that, whatever else he thought, he thought about her. He asked his good friend John to take care of her. He wanted John to become a son to her—to love her the way he did.

It is not surprising that those who, in St. Paul's words, put on "the mind of Christ" would discover that they loved her too. Though we may picture the love of Mary as a medieval development, it actually goes back to the faith's early days. Those first generations of Christians did not include Mary in their public preaching of the gospel; they did not expose her to the gaze of the world. (Likewise, a celebrity today will object if reporters take photos of his family.) But when believers were gathered together in their home community, there Mary was cherished. As new members were brought into the body of Christ, they would also begin to share in the love the Christ child had for his Mother.

How can we know her the way they did? Our primary source of information about Mary is the Scriptures, of course, but the few passages about her have been so burdened by competing interpretations that they spark more argument than illumination. Just beyond that center, however, there is a wealth of other materials that were embraced by the early Christians. You could think of it as analogous to the materials found today in a Christian bookstore: stories, prayers, artwork, and songs that help enrich the life of faith. By looking at materials pertaining to Mary that were popular in those first centuries, we can learn something about how the early Christians viewed her.

In fact, their viewpoint is valuable whenever we seek to understand Scripture. Not because these early Christians were necessarily smarter or holier than we are, but because they had this practical advantage: they were still living in the culture that produced the Christian Scriptures. The Greek of the New Testament was their daily business language. They lived in the Middle East, or along its gossipy trade routes. Their parents or great-grandparents had been alive when

Christ walked the earth. The history of these things was the history of their backyard, and some things that scholars now struggle to comprehend were as familiar and obvious as their own kitchen table.

And from the first they loved Mary—freely, deeply, and some way instinctively. This can puzzle some contemporary Christians, living as we do on the other side of centuries of controversy over Mary. It is my hope that, as we stand behind these fervent Christians and peer over their shoulders, we will be able to see what they see, and come to love her too.

We'll do that by reading three ancient texts about Mary. In each case we'll begin with some historic background, and then move to consider theological and cultural questions (sometimes, uncomfortable questions) that the document raises, before entering the complete text.

The first work is a "gospel," or a narrative of Mary's life, which begins with her conception by her mother, Anna, and continues through the birth of Jesus. It provided a kind of "prequel" to the biblical Gospels, and was extremely popular. It was in written form by AD 150, but I suspect that (like the biblical Gospels) it collected stories that were previously in oral circulation.

If these stories were originally passed along orally, we have no way of knowing how far back they might go. We can know at least that we are in the company of Christians who lived during the era of persecutions, and well before the New Testament was given final form. Yet they were already enthusiastically in love with Mary. This book was circulated widely and embraced warmly, and its popularity is reflected in the unusually high number of ancient copies and translations that have been found.

Scholars know this text by the modern title bestowed by a sixteenth-century translator: the *Protevangelium of James*. The ancient church knew it by a number of different titles, most including a reference to James as its source. I have called it the *Gospel of Mary* because today we expect a title to identify a work's contents, rather than its author. (We'll explain the use of *Lost* later on.)

The second text is a very brief prayer to Mary, found on a scrap of papyrus in Egypt about a hundred years ago. The artifact is dated at AD 250, though (as above) the prayer itself is probably older; the papyrus just represents one time it got written down.

This is the oldest known prayer to Mary. It begins with "Under your compassion . . ." and is still in use. In the Roman Catholic Church it is called *Sub tuum praesidium*, and in the Eastern Orthodox Church it is among the closing prayers of the evening services.

The third text is a lengthy, complex, and beautiful hymn written by the deacon and hymnographer St. Romanos, who was born in Syria about AD 475. This is the best-known of his works, and is regularly cited as the highest achievement of Byzantine Christian poetry. Eastern Christians are familiar with it as the *Akathist Hymn*, and they sing it during Lent, near the March 25 feast of the Annunciation (that is, the angel Gabriel's announcement to Mary that she would conceive a son). Here I am calling it the *Annunciation Hymn*, again with the aim of identifying its contents.

Many Western Christians are unfamiliar with Mary, and somewhat leery of her; they suspect that it's possible for devotion to her to get out of hand, and even eclipse the honor due to God. It is true that, over time and in other lands, praise of the Virgin that had been intended as lovingly poetic developed into something more literal, and consequently less healthy.

In Europe from the twelfth century on, strains of Marian devotion were arising that held that she could manipulate or even overrule her Son, that he was perpetually enraged but she was merciful, that she could work miracles by her own magical powers, that mechanical repetition of prayers to her guaranteed salvation, and that she had facilitated Christ's work by her presence at the Crucifixion. The effects of these mistaken ideas lingered for centuries, and have not been wholly eliminated.

But, as we will see, the early Middle Eastern church is not the medieval European church. All that sad confusion lay a thousand years from the time of the first love-notes to Mary, the time that we are entering now.

# ONE

# Telling
# Mary's Story

*James who?*

THE FIRST ANCIENT TEXT PRESENTED IN THIS BOOK, the *Gospel of Mary*, provides stories about Mary that were greatly loved in the early church. These engaging narratives cover Mary's life from her conception through the birth of Christ, and were gathered into written form sometime before AD 150. The material itself could well be older, and in a time when illiteracy was still common, it could have been passed along orally for some time before anyone transcribed it.

While today Western scholars call this the *Protevangelium of James*, in the early church it went by several different titles. The common mark was some reference to "James," since that's who claims to be the author in the book's closing words: "I, James, wrote this history."

Who is this James? There are three famous Jameses in the New Testament. The first was a member of the twelve apostles, and even a member of the trio closest to the Lord,

"Peter and James and John." He's called James the Greater. Another apostle, James the son of Alphaeus, is usually called James the Less. However, the Greek adjective *micros* may mean "younger" or "smaller," and since both were members of the Twelve, perhaps their friends called them "Big James" and "Little James" to tell them apart.

The third James is identified in Scripture as "James, the Lord's brother." He is called James the Just. This is the James who is claimed to be author of this Gospel.

This James appears several times in the New Testament. In 1 Corinthians 15, St. Paul tells us that James received a private appearance of the Resurrected Lord. In Acts 15 we see him presiding over the first church council, in his capacity as the first bishop of Jerusalem (likely the first bishop anywhere). In addition to being author of biblical Epistle of James, he is also credited with writing the oldest surviving Eucharistic liturgy, the Liturgy of St. James. This worship service was edited and condensed in the fourth century, and the shorter version, now called the Divine Liturgy of St. John Chrysostom, is still the standard Sunday worship of the Eastern Orthodox Church.

The church historian Hegesippus, writing about AD 165, says that James was respected by all and that even non-Christians called him "James the Just." He prayed so much that "his knees became calloused like those of a camel."

Hegesippus also recounts James' death. Jewish leaders, concerned at the rise of Christianity, and believing James to be a righteous and reasonable man, brought him to the summit of the Temple to address the populace. But instead of dissuading them, James preached the second coming of Christ, and many began to cry "Hosanna to the Son of David!" The Pharisees then shoved James off to the ground, where he struggled to his knees and asked God's forgiveness for those attacking him. As some took up stones to hurl at him, a launderer threw the heavy staff he used to stir the pot of boiling clothes, and it struck James a fatal wound to the head.

Tradition holds that James died in AD 62. At a press conference in 2002, the Discovery Channel and the Biblical Archeological Society presented a startling find: an ossuary that bore the inscription "James, son of Joseph, brother of Jesus." (What's an ossuary? In Jerusalem of Jesus' day there was insufficient cemetery space, so bodies were shrouded and placed in caves. When the space was later needed for other burials, the bones would be gathered and transferred into a smaller container, a "bone box.") If the empty limestone casket had truly been James' final resting place, it would be the most direct connection yet with anyone who knew Jesus during his earthly life. After examining the box, the Israeli Antiques Authority concluded that it is an authentic ossuary from the era, but that the inscription is a forgery. (Nevertheless, the ossuary still has advocates who claim it is authentic.)

## *Did our Lord have a brother?*

That is, of course, a sticky theological question. Since the Scriptures present us with the virginal conception of Christ, classic Christianity has never entertained the idea that the Greek term *adelphos* meant that James was Jesus' full brother. There have been three ways of understanding the term. James was either Jesus' step-brother, or his half-brother, or his cousin.

The earliest belief was that James is Jesus' stepbrother, the son of Joseph and a previous wife. This is the view taken by the *Gospel of Mary*, and is still held by Eastern Orthodox Christians. This would mean that James was older than Jesus, though he may still have been a child when Mary came to live in Joseph's home. She would have taken over the care of any motherless children, and they would have grown up alongside Jesus; people who knew the family would have thought of them, for all practical purposes, as Jesus' brothers and sisters. An implied claim in this gospel is that James, as older brother, was a witness to many of the events he describes. In the church known as Chora, near Constantinople, there is a magnificent series of fourteenth-century mosaics illustrating episodes from Mary's life. One shows the family on their way to Bethlehem. Pregnant Mary is seated on a donkey, with white-haired Joseph walking behind her and young James leading the way.

However, many Protestants believe instead that, after Jesus' birth, Mary and Joseph entered a normal married relationship, and James is a subsequent son. In this case, James would be Jesus' younger half-brother. But the whole topic of Mary's perpetual virginity is a challenging one, and we'll consider it later on. Even if Mary and Joseph had sub-sequent children, James could still be an older stepbrother from a previous marriage. That is how the early church knew him.

But Roman Catholics believe that James was not Joseph's son either. They follow a proposal made by St. Jerome in the fourth century, that Joseph also preserved perpetual virginity. Jerome argued therefore that James was a cousin of Jesus, the son of Mary's sister, and identified him with James the Less.

### What's Lost About It?

And that brings us to how this work got "lost." Since the *Gospel of Mary* presents Joseph as a father and a widower, rather than ever-virgin, it was not accepted in the West. The history here is hard to trace, what with the *Gospel* being known by different titles, and some supposed letters from historic characters being ancient forgeries. The Gelasian Decree of AD 492 includes the *Gospel of Mary* in the list of books "not to be received," not even for devotional reading. (But did Pope Gelasius actually write that Decree? You see how complicated it gets.)

At any rate, the *Gospel of Mary* was excluded from the Roman Catholic tradition because it shows Joseph as a widower. (And there's another element in the story that so outraged St. Jerome that he termed any work where it appears "ravings"—we'll get to that later on.) But despite official rejection of this text, many of the stories it contains entered Western Christian devotion just the same, through variations and retellings.

So "lost" means that this work was rejected and forgotten by Western Christians (as a friend comments, "Not lost, but tossed"). It doesn't mean that the scroll was dug up in the desert last week. When it comes to ancient documents, "lost" does not necessarily mean "recently found." The *Gospel of Judas*, released with much fanfare in April 2006, was actually discovered sometime in the 1970s. And portions of the *Gospel of Thomas*, the supposedly Gnostic document regularly used to challenge classic Christianity, have been around since 1898.

There has been a flood of similar "secret," "hidden," and "lost" documents lately, usually presented with the insinuation that they contain material so outrageous that the oppressive early church tried to stamp them out. (Though in the second century, when Gnosticism flourished, Christians had no such power; the oppressive Roman government was still trying to stamp them out.) But many times these ancient documents turn out to be less than the thrill they're advertised to be. Some may have gotten "lost" simply because the average Christian found them tedious.

The French Egyptologist Jean Doresse was one of the first scholars to examine the trove of Gnostic literature found near the Nile village of Nag Hammadi in 1945. In *The Secret Books of the Egyptian Gnostics* (1958), Doresse writes that these Gnostic works had been previously known only through excerpts quoted by their opponents. It was assumed that defenders of orthodoxy, like St. Irenaeus, had chosen the most ridiculous passages for critique. But "it is as though Fate had been trying to poke fun at the learned," because the intact works, now that they've been recovered, turn out to be "the most complicated and surely the most incoherent that Gnosticism ever produced." The ancient orthodox critics of these works now "look almost eulogistic, almost benevolent" in taking them "so kindly and seriously as to do them the honor of refutation."

The ancient Christian writings that rose to the top, and were eventually included in the New Testament canon, were among other things more appealing. In his review of the *Gospel of Judas* for *The New Yorker*, Adam Gopnik writes: "Simply as editors, the early Church fathers did a fine job of leaving the strong stories in and the weird ones out. The orthodox canon gives us a Christ who is convincing as a character in a way that this Gnostic one is not. . . . It is not hard to prefer [the biblical Jesus] to the Jesus of the new [Gnostic] Gospel, with his stage laughter and significant winks and coded messages . . . a know-it-all with a nimbus."

So there is the canonical New Testament on the one hand and the various non-orthodox (Gnostic and otherwise) works on the other. But there is a third category, books that the early Christians enjoyed and circulated widely, but that did not rise to the level of Scripture. (To be included in the New Testament canon it was necessary to make a convincing claim of apostolic origin, and some got in only after a fight. The Revelation of St. John and the Epistle to the Hebrews were not accepted by some communities until the late fourth century.)

This third category of ancient works takes many different forms: biographies, sermons, visions, letters, biblical

commentaries, debates with non-believers, and more. One
enduringly popular text, for example, was the collection of
seven letters written by the bishop St. Ignatius of Antioch,
as he was being taken as a prisoner to his execution in
Rome in AD 110. A more colorful text is The Shepherd,
an allegorical, dreamlike story attributed to St. Hermas
and composed around AD 140. The Didache ("Teaching"),
ascribed to the apostles, gives instructions on Christian
behavior and summarizes the rites of baptism and
Eucharist; it is often given a date between AD 65–80, roughly
the time the New Testament was being written. One of my
favorite early works is the prison journal of St. Perpetua, AD
203, in which she recorded the events, miracles, and visionary
dreams she and her companions experienced while awaiting
their death in the arena.

None of these works are very long, and all of them and
many others can be readily found in translation on the
Internet. Such early Christian writings open a new window
for those who assume that, apart from the Scriptures, we
have no record of the early Christians' lives and thinking.
On the contrary, the resources are so vast that it would be
a challenge to read them all in a lifetime. The standard
collection, containing works from the first six centuries,
takes up almost five feet of shelf space in my study: large
pages, tiny type, 38 volumes.

Though the *Gospel of Mary* was lost to the Western
Christian tradition, it was never lost in the East—on the contrary, it was enthusiastically embraced and widely circulated,
and translated into Syriac, Ethiopic, Georgian, Sahidic,

Slavonic, Armenian, and Arabic. When the nineteenth-century scholar von Tischendorf established an authoritative Greek version, he was able to draw on seventeen manuscripts; as more copies have turned up in the decades since, that figure has risen to 140. This was an unusually popular book, and Postellus, the scholar who made the translation into Latin in 1522, thought that in the East it was even being read during worship. That seems unlikely; it was not accepted as Scripture. But it's clear that many of the stories here were taken to heart very early and woven into the faith of the Christian East.

On the other hand, even though this *Gospel* has been available in English for almost 200 years, Western Christians are not likely to encounter it outside a seminary classroom. That is a loss indeed.

### *To Love a Little Girl*

This work is interesting, among other reasons, because it shows that this very early Christian community could cherish a little girl. Throughout history, the most endangered member of any human society is a newborn girl. In most traditional cultures, and some modern ones, there are social and financial advantages to a son, but a daughter is welcome only when enough sons precede her. In too many times and places a little girl has not been welcome at all, regarded as pointless trouble and a waste of food.

The results can be tragic, even today. China has an unnaturally high ratio of boys to girls (no doubt related to that nation's "one child policy"), and the vanished girls may be lost before birth by forced or sex-selection abortion, or afterwards by abandonment, infanticide, or disease. In India, sex-selection abortion is illegal, but still so prevalent that an estimated half a million unborn girls go missing every year. In the sad history of this world countless little girls have met with tragedy—unnoticed by the passing parade, but never forgotten by God.

Yet in this nearly two-thousand-year-old story from the Middle East, we see a baby girl whose birth is greeted with a cry of exultation rather than disappointment. We are told how she took her first steps, and about the big first-birthday party her father threw for her, and how the neighborhood girls played with her. In the church at Chora, mentioned above, another mosaic in the series on Mary's life expresses the tenderness of this love. It depicts Joachim and Anna seated side-by-side with baby Mary between them, and they are cuddling and kissing her as she reaches up to touch her mother's face. Above their heads the title reads "the Kolakeia of the Theotokos." *Theotokos* means "Birth-giver of God," and is a very early title for the Virgin Mary, while *kolakeia* means cherishing her with sweet, adoring words— a pastime familiar to anyone who ever loved a baby.

### Did it really happen?

Whatever we conclude about this story's historicity, its popularity shows us that very early Christians found it easy to believe that a little girl was worthy of love. That alone is refreshing, and the details that appear as the story unfolds are so charming that we feel a kinship with the story's first hearers across the centuries. When the three-year-old Mary sits down on a Temple step and "dances with her feet," it's no wonder that "all the house of Israel loved her."

What about the historicity of this story? It is certainly marked by miracles and wonders, though no more so than the pages of the New Testament. Scholars today doubt most of what happens, while some earlier generations of Christians accepted it wholeheartedly. If you can put yourself in their shoes, and manage to suspend judgment, you'll enjoy it even more.

But in an important sense historical accuracy is beside the point. The most valuable aspect of these stories for early Christians was that they show how Mary was used by God to complete his plan. These are typological stories, and they set up echoes with prophecies in the Hebrew Scriptures.

For example, the *Gospel of Mary* depicts the child entering the temple, and going even into the Holy of Holies. To say that scholars doubt this happened is an understatement. But put yourself in the place of a second-century listener. The Holy of Holies in the Jerusalem Temple was an extraordinary space: a perfect cube, 30 feet on each side. It was concealed behind a heavy embroidered curtain, and only once a year did a human being step inside. Then the High Priest would enter, bringing with him a sacrificial blood-offering. God required that the priest's steps be accompanied by the sound of bells sewn to the hem of his robes (as we're told in the book of Exodus), "lest he die."

Over a thousand years before the birth of Christ, when the children of Israel were still wandering in the desert, God gave Moses detailed instructions about the making and furnishing of the "tent of meeting." In Exodus we read that there is to be, not just a "holy place," but also a "most holy place," separated from it by a curtain. Moses was told to place in this Holy of Holies an elaborately carved and gilded chest called the Ark. Even the interior of the Ark was clad in gold, though that secret place would never be seen. The Ark was designed to hold the "testimony" of God's care for his people: the tablets of the Law given to Moses on Mt. Sinai; a golden jar of manna; and Aaron's rod, which had miraculously blossomed.

Above the Ark God commanded that Moses set two carved cherubim covered with gold, facing each other with their wings touching. And in the space above them, invisible on his "mercy seat" (Greek, *hilasterion*), God said that his presence would rest.

(Variations on that Greek term sometimes get translated "expiation" or even "propitiation," but the underlying image remains that of a place where we meet God to receive mercy. St. Paul writes to the Romans that God put Jesus forward "as a hilasterion by his blood, to be received by faith.")

We shouldn't imagine this as a place where a bargain is concluded to the satisfaction of all parties, with hand-shakes all round. It is a terrifying place. It is like leaning over the edge of a canyon and feeling the wind whip by. Any illusions about your significance are wiped away; you realize how puny and inconsequential you are. And yet the beauty is so intoxicating that you only crave more. You long to have a bigger heart that could take it all in. That's a taste of what "the fear of the Lord" means.

When Moses finished his preparations, "the cloud covered the tent of meeting, and the glory of the Lord filled the tabernacle" (Ex. 40:34), with such power that he was not able to enter it. Centuries later, when Solomon dedicated the temple he had built in Jerusalem (as we read in 1 Kings 8:10, 11), "a cloud filled the house of the Lord," and the priests could not endure its presence, "for the glory of the Lord filled the house of the Lord." And when God showed Ezekiel a vision of the future temple, "the glory of the Lord filled the temple of the Lord" (Ezek. 44:4), overwhelming Ezekiel and casting him to the ground.

When God comes to fill his tabernacle, he overshadows it with blinding glory. And when Mary asked the angel how she could conceive a son, the angel replied (in Lk. 1:35), "the Holy Spirit will come upon you, and the power of the Most High will overshadow you."

The Ark of Moses did not last. By the time it was carried into Solomon's temple, the urn of manna and Aaron's rod had been lost, and it contained only the tablets of the Law. By the time of Christ, the Ark itself had been lost. When little three-year-old Mary came into the Holy of Holies, all that dark, echoing space was empty. But the Ark it had been designed to hold was only a foreshadowing of the true Ark, who now enters in the form of a little girl.

An ancient Eastern Orthodox hymn in honor of this moment says:

Today is the prelude of God's good will
and the heralding of the salvation of mankind.
In the temple of God, the Virgin is presented openly,
and she proclaims Christ unto all.
To her, then, with a great voice let us cry aloud:
Rejoice, O fulfillment of the Creator's dispensation!

While writing this section I was corresponding with a friend who committed a catchy typo: he wrote that in this gospel "Mary enters the template." That may not be elegant, but it does indicate why these images resounded so much for the early Christians. Mary's parallels to the Ark show how, throughout history, God had been readying Creation for the coming of Christ, the one "destined before the foundation of the world" (1 Pet. 1:20).

### Purity

The *Gospel of Mary* emphasizes Mary's virginity—not only in conceiving Jesus, but also throughout the delivery. To be specific, it claims that not just the conception but also the delivery of her child did not violate her physical virginity.

This will strike many modern readers as a strange thing to say. And irrelevant as well: why would it matter? (Note that we're not discussing whether Mary remained virgin all her life, only whether she was virgin after delivering the Christ child.)

The common assumption today is that early Christians fussed about such things because they were uncomfortable with the human body, and particularly touchy about sex.

But that's anachronistic. In the Scriptures as here, material Creation is affirmed; the very idea of the Incarnation shows that a real flesh-and-blood body can bear the divine, as a candlewick bears flame.

We take this concept for granted today, but if you think what it would be like to hear it for the first time, it can be pretty disturbing. Offense at the idea that Christ really became a human being prompted alternative "spiritual" versions of the faith to spring up, the best-known being Gnosticism. (And sometimes even Christians misread St. Paul's distinction between flesh and spirit as meaning "body bad, spirit good." That idea may find a home in neo-Platonic philosophy, but not in St. Paul.)

A high respect for the physical body was why early Christians sought to gather the bloody remains of martyrs, even when it endangered them to do so. The body of a Christian is literally a temple of the Holy Spirit, and because of that it deserves honor. If these believers had been uncomfortable with the human body, they would not have treated these battered remains with such veneration, and not enclosed saint's bones within their altars.

After all, it is not the physical body that is the problem. Jesus taught that it is not what a person eats that defiles him, but rather what comes out of his mouth and heart. He explained that the damage inside a human being is integral, like a sickly tree that cannot bear good fruit. So sin is not so much a culpable deed as a self-inflicted wound. The "passions" that impel us to act out our brokenness are, in Greek, *pathon*, sufferings. The singular is *pathos*.

The way to healing is to "Be transformed by the renewal of your *nous*," as St. Paul wrote to the Romans. The New Testament word nous is usually translated "mind," but there's really no good English equivalent. It means the perceiving faculty inside a person, the "eye of the soul," which is, like a radio, designed to "tune in" to God. When the nous is centered in God, the whole person is calm and loving. When your eye is healthy, Jesus said, your whole body will be full of light.

But after Adam's fall, the nous no longer readily perceives the light of Christ permeating all Creation. The darkened nous malfunctions, and renders humans fearful and selfish, alienated from this good earth and from each other. It is habitually distracted, and in that scattered state reacts to life like a pinball colliding with silvery bumpers.

The cure is to cultivate a habit of humility and love for others—that is, repentance (in biblical Greek, *metanoia*, a transformation of the nous). The classic spiritual exercises— fasting, loving others, and prayer "without ceasing"—are the "workout routine" for reorienting the nous to abide in God. (This is explored more fully in my book *The Illumined Heart: The Ancient Christian Path of Transformation*.)

Thus, there is no ancient Christian rejection of our physical bodies or this abundant earth. If anything, that culture was less squeamish about basic functions than we are today. In this story, the priests deliberate matter-of-factly about what to do when young Mary is due to begin having periods. There are plenty of frank references to breastfeeding: "Hear, hear you twelve tribes of Israel: Anna is nursing a baby!" At the end of her labor, Mary says bluntly, "That which is within me presses me to come forth." (Compare that with a more fanciful text written about the same time, "The Ascension of Isaiah." Here Mary, after two months of pregnancy, suddenly sees a baby appear—and then discovers she is no longer pregnant.) Mary's post-birth virginity is verified the only way it could be, in a passage that apparently did not shock or offend devout original hearers.

And when Joachim and Anna receive separate promises from God that they will have a child, Anna runs to greet her husband with a hug around the neck, and we are told that he then spends the day at home. The image of their meeting, and even franker ones that depict the couple standing and embracing in front of their bed, became popular in Christian art. Mary was, after all, conceived in the usual way.

The custom of celebrating both the conception and the birth of certain figures (for example, the Annunciation of Christ's conception is observed March 25, and his birth December 25), indicates that early Christians had an adequate idea of how conception takes place and how long gestation lasts. It also shows that they believed that a new individual, a specific person, is present from the moment of conception: a person begins when his body begins. The body is not just a regrettable container. (Aristotle's view that the body and soul are separate, and that the body receives the soul at 40 or 80 days, was never accepted in the Christian East.)

Privacy was harder to come by in that ancient world, and ordinary body processes were thoroughly familiar—perhaps even more so than today, for there may be some readers who are not quite sure what "physical virginity" means. (It was no mystery to the ancient Hebrews, as we see from the startling passage in Deuteronomy 22, where a bride's parents are expected to preserve proof of their daughter's virginity so they can present it if challenged.)

The virginal conception of Christ was part of Christian preaching from the first, and a difficult part it was. Virginal birth would have no particular appeal to the first audience for the *Gospel of Mary* message, the Jews; they did not expect the Messiah to be born of a virgin, any more than they expected him to die on a cross. When Christians presented this claim they opened themselves to charges that they were fabricating a preposterous and pointless myth.

What's more, their admission that Mary's husband was not her child's father invited the obvious charge that he was "born of fornication" (as Jesus' challengers jeer in the John 8). There was no rhetorical advantage to claiming a virgin birth for Jesus, and the likeliest reason the early Christians stood by it so stoutly was that they believed it was true.

But why would Mary have to be still virgin immediately after the birth? As above, there's no rhetorical advantage, and if anything it would have been another tough sell. It seems the Christians simply believed it was true, and tried to understand God's purpose. Gregory of Nyssa (AD 335–394) proposed that the pain of childbirth is one of the bitter consequences of the Fall (as God warned Eve, "In pain you shall bring forth children"). When God acts to reverse that damage, every element will be joy: "It was indeed necessary that the mother of life conceive her child with joy, and perfect her act of giving birth in joy." Gregory sees in this another miraculous proof of God's sovereignty. Just as the bush Moses saw was filled with the blazing presence of God yet not destroyed, so Mary's bodily integrity was not altered by childbirth.

### *Ever-Virgin?*

Though the *Gospel of Mary* shows her as a virgin before and after the birth of Christ, it does not comment on whether she remained a virgin all her life. That was the consensus of the early church, however, and it was universally believed until recent centuries. Even some Reformation leaders, including Ulrich Zwingli and Martin Luther, upheld it. Though many Christians today assume Mary and Joseph entered normal marital relations after Jesus' birth, that belief was not accepted by any orthodox Christian writer for over 1500 years.

In the fourth century, a rare attempt to advance this view was made by a writer named Helvidius. He offered as evidence Matthew 1:25: "[Joseph] knew her not until she had borne a son." Surely that meant Joseph "knew" Mary after the birth of Jesus, Helvidius said.

We know of Helvidius only through St. Jerome's indignant rebuttal. Jerome fired back that, if we say, "Helvidius did not repent until his death," it doesn't mean he repented afterwards. What's more (waxing sarcastic, which Jerome could certainly do), if "until" means normal marital relations began after the birth of Christ, on what grounds could Helvidius allow even a moment's delay? Midwives would have to bustle the child out of the room "while the husband clasps his exhausted wife."

This "until" did not trouble early Christians, who understood it to mean "before." Matthew consistently tells the story of Mary's pregnancy from Joseph's point of view, and is here restating that Joseph had no part in Jesus' conception. Likewise, Luke's reference to "her first-born son" (in Luke 2) is a formula indicating inheritance status, and requires no subsequent sons. "Every male that opens the womb shall be called holy to the Lord."

The strongest evidence that Mary had no other sons is that the crucified Jesus consigned her to John's care (John 19:26–27). This makes sense if Jesus' death was going to leave her unprotected, but not if it meant wresting her from the home of biological sons.

Apart from Helvidius, only Tertullian (who was less than fully orthodox; Jerome dismisses him as "not of the Church") proposed that Mary entered an ordinary married life with Joseph. Tertullian saw in this a blessing of both the virgin and the married state. But the remainder of the early Christian writers are united in upholding her life-long virginity—an assertion, similar to the virgin birth above, that would be unnecessary, and awkward to defend, and thus unlikely to be invented, if it were not believed true.

### Restoring an Icon

The version in this book is my own production, made by applying my rusty Greek skills to the text with a dictionary on one hand and a half-dozen English translations, old and new, on the other. I began to sense what an honor it is to handle an ancient text like this, which has been so beloved over the millennia. It tells an old, old story about the Virgin Mary, and in a sense it is an ancient icon of her, rendered in words rather than wood and paint. In producing this version, I was able to be like an iconographer who makes a copy of an ancient icon, and passes the image forward to new generations. I hope I have done it justice, and allowed the essential charm of the story to shine through.

You'll notice that, as this *Gospel* retells the story of Christ's conception and birth, it omits some details that appear in the Bible. Mary does not sing "My soul magnifies the Lord" after Elizabeth praises her pregnancy; there is a manger, but not an inn; there are Magi, but not shepherds. However, similar gaps appear in the biblical accounts: St. Matthew alone knows the story of the Magi, while St. Luke is our sole source for the Annunciation.

These gaps reinforce for me the feeling that the *Gospel of Mary* has folk origins. Journalists like to say that they write "the first draft of history," but the first draft of history is, in fact, not written; it's told aloud, carried from one person to the next, in bits and snatches, bearing differing emphases depending on the teller. Some communities will have pieces of the story that others don't; different versions may bear the names of different original sources or eyewitnesses. Some time would pass before anything was written down at all. Every story will, of necessity, have some omissions; if one tried to tell everything Jesus did, as St. John says at the end of his Gospel, the world could not contain all the books that would be required.

Slowing down to read word-for-word in Greek impressed me, among other things, with how much this resembles an oral, rather than written, story. In his landmark work *Orality and Literacy*, Walter Ong explains that, in an illiterate culture, works are organized in ways that make them easier to put together on the spot from memory. Songs or poems are likely to be marked by patterns of repetition, rather than rhythm or rhyme; we see this in the Psalms and Proverbs, and here in Anna's lament in 3:2–3.

Repetitiveness in the narrative itself, and not just in poetic sections, is another common feature of material delivered orally. You'll remember from your pre-literate childhood days that hearing certain familiar lines in a fairy tale reappear was one of the pleasures of listening to the story. This gospel uses, in addition to stock phrases like "as the Lord God lives," plain old repetition to a degree that most readers find ample. What constitutes excellent oral technique, wears a bit thin when turned into written text. So I have given the work some light ironing (no starch), aiming to clarify points that would be obscure while not obscuring the directness and clarity of the original.

One good earmark of oral origin is a habitual use of *and* to link elements together—"and he did this, and he went there, and he said that." (The Greek word is *kai*, and this verbal habit goes by the grand name *kai parataxis*.) This is the way people talk, rather than how they write, because hearers absorb information best in short bursts. The earliest biblical Gospel, that of St. Mark, is knit together with "kai"s, and among the four Gospels most closely resembles something that was previously in spoken form.

This *Gospel of Mary* fairly swarms with "kai"s. Of the roughly 4300 words in the Greek text, 440 are "kai." (I've removed a fair amount of them for this English version, but you can get a sample of the original in chapter 19.)

All this suggests that this tale was not composed outright by an audacious and imaginative second-century novelist. Rather, it was snatched from the air of oral tradition, perhaps in bits and pieces, and the origin of the story itself is lost in the mists of the first century of Christian history.

# The Gospel of Mary

*The Gospel of Mary*

1 This story opens abruptly, with a reference to a book called *The Histories of the Twelve Tribes of Israel,* a work unknown to scholars. It also launches right into telling us what Joachim is doing, without pausing to tell us who he is (he is, or will be, Mary's father). This entire "Gospel" is a branch springing from the greater "gospel," and assumes that hearers already know who Jesus is and what he has done, that they know the name of his mother, and even the name of his grandfather. We are plunged immediately into the midst of a circle of listeners who love the Lord and are eager to hear more of the story.

2 Not the final Day of Judgment (Joel 2:11), obviously. Perhaps this refers to the conclusion of the Feast of Tabernacles, as described in the Gospel of St. John: "the last day of the feast, the great day" (Jn. 7:37).

3 This was probably just an ugly outburst; there was no rule denying the childless the right to make offerings. (Reuben is not identified as a priest, and may have just been a rude interloper.) But in the Scriptures we do see a sad pattern of deriding and shaming those who have not borne children. The wives of the patriarch Jacob, Leah and Rachel, compete bitterly to supply him with a son (Genesis 29–30). It is pitiful to see Leah hoping that her abundance of offspring would make her husband love her as much as he did her prettier sister.

  Similarly, though Hannah was the favorite of her husband, Elkanah, she was tormented by his other wife, Peninnah. As we read in the book of Samuel: "Her rival used to provoke [Hannah] sorely, to irritate her, because the LORD had closed her womb." On such occasions Hannah would weep and refuse to eat, though her husband assured her, "Am I not more to you than ten sons?" When the priest Eli sees Hannah in the temple, speaking to God under her breath, he takes her for a mumbling drunk. But when Hannah explains, "I have been pouring out my soul before the LORD," he promises an answer to her prayer. The child she would bear became the great prophet Samuel (1 Sam. 1:1–28).

CHAPTER 1

1. In the histories of the twelve tribes of Israel it is written that Joachim was extremely rich.[1] He always brought to the Lord a double portion of his gifts, saying to himself, "From my over-abundance I give an offering for all the people, and for myself, a mercy-offering for the forgiveness of the Lord God."

2. Now the great day of the Lord was drawing near,[2] and the children of Israel were bringing in their gifts. But Reuben stood in front of Joachim, saying, "It's not right for you to be first to offer your gifts, for you have not begotten any seed in Israel!"[3]

4 The name "Isaac" means "laughter," and Abraham laughed when he first heard that a son would be born to him. "Abraham fell on his face and laughed, and said to himself, 'Shall a child be born to a man who is a hundred years old? Shall Sarah, who is ninety years old, bear a child?'" But God repeated, "I will establish my covenant with Isaac, whom Sarah shall bear to you at this season next year" (Gen. 17:17, 21).

5 Periods of forty days and nights have special significance in the Scriptures. That is the length of time that rain fell during the flood, the time that Moses spent on Mt. Sinai, and the time that Christ fasted in the wilderness, among many other examples. Joachim's words here recall those of Jesus: "My food is to do the will of him who sent me" (John 4:34).

3. Joachim was very grieved. He went into the record of the twelve tribes of the people, saying, "I will see if I alone have not begotten seed in Israel." And so he searched, but he found that all the righteous had raised up seed in Israel. Then Joachim remembered the patriarch Abraham, and how even in the closing days of his life God had given him a son, Isaac.[4]

4. And Joachim was exceedingly grieved. He did not show himself to his wife, but right away took himself into the wilderness. He pitched a tent and determined to fast for forty days and forty nights. He said to himself, "I will not go down, not for food nor for drink, until the Lord my God looks upon me. Prayer will be my food and drink."[5]

6 Just like Joachim, Anna comes into the story suddenly and without introduction, as if it's presumed that the hearers already know who she is. In our era of vast, faceless anonymity, it's easy to forget what a small world the Holy Land then was. Everyone could be placed in a context, precisely pegged to one twig or another of a well-known family tree. The genealogies of Jesus given in the opening chapters of the Gospels of St. Matthew and St. Luke are just a blur of names to us today, but at the time they were written it was the genealogical equivalent of citing longitude and latitude.

Jesus didn't suddenly appear from a glittering haze, but grew up under the gaze of a specific village and a particular family line. "Is not this the carpenter's son? Is not his mother called Mary?" the citizens of Nazareth ask, naming his stepbrothers (or half-brothers) and fixing him firmly in the social grid. They grumble, "Where then did this man get all this?"

How can someone so familiar be so extraordinary? Either be a god and flash out like lightning, or be a regular guy. This unexpected combination provokes nothing so much as resentment. It would have been easier for the early Christians if they had gone the "I don't know, he just showed up" route. Instead they were cheerfully transparent about Jesus' earthly origins and specific about times and places. Their confidence is audacious. Apparently they expected that eyewitnesses would support rather than hurt their cause.

And Christ's Incarnation, as unimaginable as it was in cosmic terms, was also exactly this real: his grandmother was named Anna.

7 Though Anna in her grief had spoken sharply to Judith, she must have respected her servant's opinion, because she now tries to follow her advice. "The ninth hour" is three o'clock in the afternoon.

8 Those familiar with bay laurels may doubt that you can sit underneath one, since the cultivated plant is usually kept to the size of a shrub, but it can grow to 60 feet. A crown of laurel leaves was a sign of victory in ancient Greece, and fragrant bay leaves are still used in cooking.

9 Sarah, like Abraham, laughed at the preposterous news that she would have a son in old age. "The LORD said, 'I will surely

## CHAPTER 2

1. His wife, Anna, sang two dirges and mourned two lamentations, saying: "I will grieve for my widowhood, and I will grieve for my childlessness."[6]

2. The great day of the Lord was drawing near, and Judith, her maidservant, said to her: "How long will you humble your soul? For, behold, the great day of the Lord is coming, and it is not lawful for anyone to mourn. Instead, take this festive headband that was given to me by the woman who creates such work. It's not right for me to wear it because I am only a servant, and it bears a royal insignia."

3. And Anna cried, "Get away from me! I won't have such things! It is the Lord himself who has so greatly humbled me. Perhaps some evildoer gave this to you, and you've come to make me share in your sin!" And Judith said, "Why should I curse you, because you won't listen to my voice? It is the Lord God who has shut your womb, so that you cannot bear fruit in Israel."

4. Anna was exceedingly grieved, but she put off her mourning garments, washed her face and hair, and put on her wedding garments.[7] At about the ninth hour she went down to walk in her garden. She saw a laurel tree and sat down under it,[8] and implored the Lord, saying, "O God of my fathers, bless me and listen to my prayer, just as you blessed the womb of Sarah and gave her a son, Isaac."[9]

return to you in the spring, and Sarah your wife shall have a son.' And Sarah was listening at the tent door behind him. Now Abraham and Sarah were old, advanced in age; it had ceased to be with Sarah after the manner of women. So Sarah laughed to herself, saying, 'After I have grown old, and my husband is old, shall I have pleasure?' The LORD said to Abraham, 'Why did Sarah laugh, and say, "Shall I indeed bear a child, now that I am old?" Is anything too hard for the LORD? At the appointed time I will return to you, in the spring, and Sarah shall have a son.' But Sarah denied, saying, 'I did not laugh'; for she was afraid. He said, 'No, but you did laugh'" (Gen. 18:10–15).

10 In Anna's lament, as in the biblical Psalms, a song is distinguished from ordinary speech by repetition rather than rhythm or rhyme. Any work that exists primarily in oral rather than written form (and all works, in cultures where literacy is not common) is composed of standardized elements that are easy to recall. This is why Goldilocks has the same proportion-related complaint about each item she encounters in the three Bears' home.

11 Anna's song alludes to Psalm 1:3: "He is like a tree planted by streams of water, that yields its fruit in its season."

CHAPTER 3

1. Looking up toward heaven, Anna saw a sparrow's nest in the laurel tree. Immediately she began to lament within herself, "Oh, what father begot me, and what mother brought me forth? For I was born only to be cursed before the children of Israel, and reproached, and mockingly cast out of the temple of my God.

2. "Oh, what am I like? I am not like the birds of the heavens, for even the birds are fruitful before you, Lord. Oh, what am I like? I am not like the unreasoning beasts, for even the unreasoning beasts are fruitful before you, Lord.[10]

3. "Oh, what am I like? I am not like these waters, for even the waters are fruitful before you, Lord. Oh, what am I like? I am not like the earth, because the earth bears its fruit in season,[11] and blesses you, Lord."

12 "As the Lord my God lives." This phrase is used frequently in the Hebrew Scriptures to make a vow, or to emphasize a statement's veracity. When Elijah asked the widow of Zarephath for some bread, she replied, "As the LORD your God lives, I have nothing baked" (1 Kings 17:12).

13 Here Anna emulates Hannah, who endured long years of barrenness. Hannah "vowed a vow and said, 'O LORD of hosts, if thou wilt indeed look on the affliction of thy maidservant, and remember me, and not forget thy maidservant, but wilt give to thy maidservant a son, then I will give him to the LORD all the days of his life'"(1 Sam. 1:11). Anna does not specify a son or daughter, and her use of the neuter "it" is startling in English.

14 "And behold . . ." We see through Anna's eyes how handsome her returning husband looks, surrounded by his abundant flocks. The sweetness of love between old lovers is something a youth-centered culture can hardly imagine. For some of them, at least, it will come as a nice surprise.

15 Traditional icons portray various elements of this story: Anna and Joachim receiving the news from their separate angels, the couple's joyous meeting at the gate, and even the couple in their bedroom, standing and embracing in front of an inviting bed, tipped toward the viewer.

16 This is day that Mary was conceived, by tradition December 9, while her birth is a tidy nine months later, on September 8. Her conception has been observed as a feast in the Christian East since the sixth century, though in the West it was rarely noted before the eleventh century. That was when an Anglo-Saxon monk, Eadmer, proposed that the day of Mary's conception deserves honor because she was conceived without Original Sin. (For some reason, the feast is observed a day earlier in the West, on December 8.) This is what is meant by the "Immaculate Conception"—the term refers to Anna's conception of Mary, not Mary's virginal conception of Jesus.

## CHAPTER 4

1. And behold, an angel of the Lord stood there, saying, "Anna, Anna, the Lord God has heard your prayer. You will conceive and bear, and your child will be spoken of in all the inhabited world." Then Anna said, "As the Lord my God lives,[12] whether I bear a boy or a girl, I will bring it as an offering to the Lord my God, and it will minister to him all the days of its life."[13]

2. Then there came two angels saying to her, "Look, Joachim your husband is coming with his flocks." For an angel of the Lord had gone down to him saying, "Joachim, Joachim, the Lord God has heard your prayer. Go down from here; behold, Anna your wife will conceive in her womb."

3. And Joachim immediately came down and called his shepherds, saying, "Bring here to me twelve pure, spotless lambs for an offering to the Lord my God; and bring twelve pure, spotless calves for the priests and elders; and bring me a hundred goats, which will be for all the people."

4. And behold, Joachim was coming with his flocks.[14] Anna was standing by the gate, and she saw Joachim coming. And Anna ran and threw her arms around his neck,[15] saying, "Now I know that the Lord God has blessed me exceedingly! For the widow is no longer a widow, and the childless woman conceives in her womb!" And Joachim went into his house and rested that first day.[16]

The Immaculate Conception of Mary was defined as dogma
by Pope Pius IX in 1854. It is not a belief shared by the Christian
East, due in part to a different understanding of the effects of
Adam and Eve's sin.

17 In Exodus 28:36–38, the Lord instructs Moses to make a plate
of gold and inscribe upon it "Holy to the LORD," and attach it
to the priest's headpiece. By this, "Aaron shall take upon himself any guilt incurred" by those making offerings unworthily.

18 Icons show Anna reclining in bed in a handsomely appointed
room, attended by women who fan her, offer medicines, hold her
hand, and test the warmth of the newborn's bathwater. A carved
wooden cradle on rockers waits nearby. It is very different from
the humble setting in which her daughter will give birth.

19 A woman was considered unclean from the beginning of labor
until fourteen days after the birth of a daughter, and during that
time she was not to touch her husband or anything holy.
Breastfeeding, however, would begin immediately, something
this verse's awkward syntax does not make clear.

20 Mary is a common name, but nevertheless difficult to translate;
one German scholar identified seventy possible meanings. But
when the root is used as a proper noun in the Hebrew
Scriptures, it means "bitter." In Ruth 1:20, after Naomi has lost
her husband and her sons, she cries, "Do not call me Naomi
[Pleasant]; call me Mara [Bitter], for the Almighty has dealt very
bitterly with me." The same name is heard in an incident during
the years that the Israelites followed Moses in the wilderness.
After three days without water they found some that was too
bitter to drink, so they called the place Marah. But God showed
Moses a certain tree and told him to throw it in, and after that
the water was sweetened and made drinkable (Ex. 15:23–25).
  It's hard to imagine how "Bitter" could become a commonly
used name for a child. No doubt many a woman, under
pressure to produce sons, found the birth of a girl-child to
be a bitter thing. And in the midst of Christ's victory we hear

## CHAPTER 5

1. The next day, when Joachim was presenting his offerings, he said to himself, "If the Lord God will be gracious to me, he will make the plate on the priest's headpiece shine out clearly to me."[17] So Joachim offered his gifts. He looked closely at the priest's headpiece as he went up to the altar of the Lord, but he could find no sin reflected there. And Joachim said, "Now I know that the Lord God has been gracious to me and forgiven all my sins." And he went down out of the temple of the Lord having been made righteous, and went into his house, rejoicing and glorifying God.

2. The months of Anna's pregnancy were fulfilled, and in the ninth month she gave birth.[18] Anna said to the midwife, "What have I borne?" and she answered, "A girl." Anna said, "This day my soul is magnified," and she laid the child in a cradle. The days of Anna's cleansing were fulfilled and she gave her breast to the child.[19] And she called her by the name Mary.[20]

this small note of tragedy, the echo in his mother's name. Mary herself knew sorrow, as the prophet Simeon had told her when she was still a joyous young mother: "A sword will pierce through your own soul also" (Lk. 2:35).

The Christian story does not ignore tragedy, but confronts and transforms it. The same God who used a tree to sweeten bitter water would one day choose another tree, the site of his Son's death as well as his glory. By it, all bitterness is turned to joy.

21 The Greek verb here is ambivalent; it might be translated "diverted." It could mean that the girls "led her aside," a euphemism indicating that they took care of her toilet training. Elijah uses it when he mocks the priests of Baal, whose god is ignoring their supplications: "Cry aloud . . .; either he is musing, or he has gone aside" (1 Kings 18:27).

22 From these descriptions of the tender care the child Mary received we can infer the flavor of the love that early Christians felt for her. Similar stories did not circulate about the infancy of other admired biblical characters, like St. Paul or St. Peter. Early believers felt a distinctive yearning to cherish Mary and communicate their love to her, and these passages provided a vicarious opportunity to do so.

## CHAPTER 6

1. And day by day the child grew stronger. When Mary was six months old, her mother set her on the ground, to test whether she could stand. She took seven steps and came back into her mother's bosom. And Anna caught her up, saying, "As my Lord God lives, you will not walk on this earth again until I bring you into the temple of the Lord." She made a sanctuary in her bedroom and would let nothing common or unclean pass through it. And she called the undefiled daughters of the Hebrews, and they played with her.[21]

2. When the child became one year old, Joachim made a great feast, and he invited the priests and the scribes and the elders and all the people of Israel. He brought Mary to the priests and they blessed her, saying, "O God of our Fathers, bless this child and give her a name of eternal renown, throughout all generations." The people responded, "Let it be so, let it be so, amen!" Then Joachim brought the child to the high priests, and they blessed her, saying, "O God most high, look upon this child and bless her with an everlasting blessing that shall never be overcome."[22]

3. And Anna carried her into the sanctuary of her bedroom; and giving her breast to the child, Anna sang a song to the Lord God, saying: "I will sing a hymn unto the Lord my God, for he has looked upon me and taken away from me

23 "Fruit of his righteousness." This phrase is echoed in Proverbs 11:30, Amos 6:12, Hebrews 12:11, and James 3:18. "Unique and yet abundant," however, is a guess at something that perplexes all translators. In Greek it seems to say, "of a single kind, and of many kinds" (*mono-ousion* and *poly-ousion*).

24 Anna's words recall those of Sarah: "Who would have said to Abraham that Sarah would suckle children? Yet I have borne him a son in his old age" (Gen. 21:7).

the reproach of my enemies. He has given me the fruit of his righteousness, unique and yet abundant.[23] Who will announce to the children of Reuben that Anna is nursing a baby? Hear, hear, you twelve tribes of Israel: Anna is nursing a baby!"[24] She then laid the child down to sleep in the bedchamber of the sanctuary, and went to serve her guests. And when the dinner was completed they went away, rejoicing and glorifying the God of Israel.

25 Readers immersed in the New Testament reflexively think of temple leaders as opponents of Christianity. In this Gospel, however, we see them acting kindly and welcoming Mary into the house of the Lord.

26 It's hard to believe that the priests would have accepted a three-year-old girl and allowed her to reside in the temple. There is the example of Samuel, however, who was presented to the priest Eli as soon as he was weaned, maybe even younger than three. When Hannah presents her son to the priest Eli, she explains that she had made this vow before the child was conceived.

This is certainly an odd idea, to hand a priest a baby and saddle him with its upbringing. Was this a well-known practice, or did Hannah come up with the idea on her own? And if she did, did other women who heard this story over the centuries believe it sanctioned by Scripture, and do the same? The pressure on barren women was intense, and many kinds of vows were no doubt made. Some women no doubt followed Hannah's example, and some of the children born would have been female. What happened then?

Could a boy, but not a girl, be allowed to live in the temple? Though certain areas were off-limits to women, St. Luke tells us of the prophetess Anna, who greeted Mary and Joseph when they came to offer doves for Jesus' birth. This widow had been living there for decades, and "she did not depart from the temple, worshiping with fasting and prayer night and day" (Lk. 2:36–38). She presents an early example of the kind of dedicated prayerful life that will be explored later by monastics and anchorites.

## Chapter 7

1. The child's months were added to her, and when she became two years old Joachim said, "Let us take her up to the temple of the Lord so that we can fulfill what we have promised, lest the Lord inquire of us and find our offerings unacceptable." Anna said, "Let us wait until she is three; otherwise, she will keep looking for her mother and father." Joachim said, "Amen, let us do so."

2. When Mary turned three Joachim said, "Call the undefiled daughters of the Hebrews, and let each one take a lamp, and let it be burning,  so that the child will not turn back and her heart be captured from the temple of the Lord." And they did this, and went up into the temple of the Lord. There the priest welcomed Mary and kissed her,[25] and blessed her saying, "The Lord has magnified your name to all generations of the earth. By you, unto the last of days, the Lord God will reveal redemption to the children of Israel."[26]

3. Then he sat her down on the third step of the altar, and the Lord God poured out grace upon her. And she danced with her feet, and all the house of Israel loved her.

27 Leviticus 15:19–33 specifies that anyone with a bodily discharge,
male or female, becomes ritually unclean, and must not touch
holy things. As Mary nears puberty, the priests discuss this
possibility frankly.

28 The specifications for the high priest's robe are recorded in
the book of Exodus; it was to be embroidered in blue, purple,
and scarlet and have bells around the hem, which "shall be
heard when he goes in to the holy place before the LORD, and
when he comes out, lest he die" (Ex. 28:35). God gave
detailed instructions to Moses regarding the appointments of
the tabernacle, requiring gold, precious stones, and elaborate
craftsmanship—even though the children of Israel were still
refugees, traveling through the wilderness and living in tents.
Beauty is such an important element in opening hearts to God
that it could not be put off for some more convenient time. In
the resonant words of the King James Version, "O worship the
LORD in the beauty of holiness" (1 Chr. 16:29; Ps. 29:2, 96:9).

29 In Numbers 17:1–9, God tells Moses to gather all the men's
staffs and place them in the tent of meeting. Aaron's staff alone
sprouts with blossoms and almonds, a sign that his family, that
of Levi, will be the priestly line.

## CHAPTER 8

1. Her parents went down marveling and praising God that the child did not turn back. Mary lived like a nurtured dove in the temple, and received food from the hand of an angel.

2. But when she reached twelve years, the priests took counsel saying, "Behold, Mary has become twelve years old in the temple of the Lord. What therefore shall we do with her, lest it come upon her as with women, and she defile the sanctuary of the Lord?"[27] They said to the high priest, "You stand before the altar of the Lord; go in and pray about her, and whatever the Lord God reveals to you, that we will do."

3. So the high priest went into the Holy of Holies bearing the vestment with twelve bells[28] and prayed concerning her. And behold, an angel of the Lord stood before him saying, "Zacharias, Zacharias, go out and call together the widowers among the people, and let each one carry his staff,[29] and the one upon whom Lord shows a sign, he shall have her as his wife." So the heralds went out into all the countryside of Judea, and the trumpet of the Lord was sounded, and all came running.

30 Joseph, like Joachim and Anna, is brought into the story with no introduction; the audience would already know his name, and that he was a carpenter.

31 A later and better-known variation on this story is that Joseph's staff budded with lilies; in the Christian West, this is understood as an emblem of his virginity.

32 Korah, Dathan, and Abiram mounted a revolt against Moses in the wilderness, and met a terrible end (the story is told in Numbers 16).

33 Some years elapse between this point and the next incident. Mary must have been 12 or 13 when she leaves the Temple for Joseph's home; when the angel appears and interrupts her while she is spinning thread for the Temple curtain, she is 16. Joseph must have continued to make trips for the sake of his construction business during these years, leaving Mary to care for any stepchildren remaining in the home.

## CHAPTER 9

1. Joseph also threw down his axe[30] and ran to the gathering, and when all had assembled they went in to the high priest. He took the staffs of them all and went into the temple and prayed. When he finished the prayer, he came out and gave each man his own staff, but there was no sign on them. The last to receive his staff was Joseph, and behold, a dove flew out of the staff and perched upon Joseph's head.[31] The high priest said to him, "You have been called to receive the virgin of the Lord. Receive her into your own keeping."

2. But Joseph spoke against this, saying, "I have sons and I am an old man, but she is a young girl. I will appear a laughingstock to the children of Israel." The priest said to him, "Joseph, fear the Lord God and remember what he did to Dathan and Kore and Abiron,[32] how the earth split open and swallowed them all, because of their rebelliousness. And now fear, Joseph, lest such things happen to your house."

3. So Joseph fearfully took her into his care. He said to her, "Mary, behold, I have received you out of the temple of the Lord my God, and now I am leaving you in my home, for I must go and work at building my houses. I will return to you quickly. May the Lord God take care of you."[33]

34 The high priest, Zacharias, includes Mary among the virgins, even though she has been betrothed to Joseph and living in his home for several years. According to tradition he counted her among the virgins even after childbirth; this offended the pious and was a contributing factor to his martyrdom.

35 Zacharias and his wife Elizabeth were also elderly and childless. When an angel appeared to Zacharias in the temple and announced that his wife would conceive a son to be named John ("the Baptist" in the West, "the Forerunner" in the East), Zacharias doubted. "[Zacharias] said to the angel, 'How shall I know this? For I am an old man, and my wife is advanced in years.' And the angel answered him, 'I am Gabriel, who stand in the presence of God; and I was sent to speak to you, and to bring you this good news. And behold, you will be silent and unable to speak until the day that these things come to pass, because you did not believe my words'" (Lk. 1:18–20). So "Zacharias fell silent" tells us that this is when John was conceived.

## CHAPTER 10

1. Now there was a council of the priests, and they said, "Let us make a veil for the temple of the Lord." So the high priest said, "Call to me the undefiled virgins of the house of David," and the officers went out and found seven. Then the high priest remembered that Mary was from the house of David and was pure,[34] so the officers went out and brought her. So they brought them into the temple of the Lord, and the high priest said, "Cast lots here before me, to know who will weave the gold, the white, the linen, the silk, the hyacinth-blue, the scarlet, and the true purple threads." And the lot fell to Mary to weave the scarlet and the true purple, and she took them and went back to her house. It was at this time that Zacharias fell silent.[35]

*We now enter a timeline that will stretch approximately 18 months. The feast of the conception of John the Baptist is observed on September 23 (and the feast of his birth on June 24), so we are at the end of September.*

36 The virgins are taking part in making a new curtain to set apart the Holy of Holies. The final creation would be an immense square, measuring 30 feet on each side. This is the curtain that was "torn in two, from top to bottom" at the moment Jesus took his last breath (Mt. 27:51). A mighty human being could perhaps have torn it from the bottom some ways upward. There is only one force that could tear it from the top.

37 "Rejoice, favored one, the Lord is with you" are the words the angel spoke to Mary, as recorded in the first chapter of Luke. *Xaire* was a standard greeting, and is often translated "Hail," but literally means "Rejoice." The next term, "favored one" resonates with it pleasingly in Greek; the verb is *xarito'o*, which is in the family of *xaris*, meaning favor, grace, or gift.

38 In Hebrew the name Joshua (which becomes *Iesus* in Greek) means "Yah [Yahweh] Saves."

39 In Luke's Gospel, Mary responds with the same words: "Behold, I am the handmaid of the Lord; let it be to me according to your word." Gabriel's announcement to Mary is known as "the Annunciation." It is the feast of the conception of Jesus, of course, and is observed on March 25. As with the prior conceptions of Mary and John, birth follows in 9 months—in this case, on Christmas, December 25.

## CHAPTER 11

1. Mary was spinning the scarlet thread she had taken.[36] And taking a pitcher, she went out to fill it with water. And a voice sounded: "Rejoice, favored one, the Lord is with you. Blessed are you among women."[37] Mary looked around to the right and the left to see where the voice was coming from. And beginning to tremble, she went back into the house and set down the pitcher. Taking up the purple thread, she sat on a chair and again began spinning.

2. And, behold, an angel of the Lord stood before her. He said, "Do not fear, Mary, for you have found grace before God, and from his Word you will conceive." Hearing this she considered in herself, and said, "Shall I conceive by the living God, and bring forth as all women bear children?"

3. And the angel said to her, "Not so, Mary; for the power of the Lord will overshadow you and the holy one born from you will be called the Son of the Most High. And you will call his name Jesus, for he will save the people from their sins."[38] And Mary said, "Behold, I am the handmaid of the Lord; let it be to me according to your word."[39]

40 Characters who are throwing, running, exclaiming and react-
ing emotionally (see Joseph's unrestrained response to Mary's
pregnancy, below) add drama to a story that has been shaped
by oral performance. For similar reasons, the evangelist Mark
uses the word "immediately" with great frequency in his
Gospel, to keep hearers on the edge of their seats. When the
action is particularly tense the synonyms pile high: "And
[Salome] came *immediately with haste* to the king and asked,
saying, 'I want you to give me *at once* the head of John the
Baptist on a platter'" (Mk. 6:25; emphasis added).

41 Luke also recounts this event. Six months have passed since
the start of the curtain project, and Elizabeth's pregnancy (and
Zacharias' silence) began. It is late March or early April. The
baby leaping in Elizabeth's womb is six months old, while
Mary is newly pregnant.

42 The Greek word is usually translated "forget," but it's not
likely such an event would slip a person's mind. Mary
says "all generations will call me blessed," which sounds like
she remembers the angel's message in 11:1. The verb can
encompass other meanings, like "overlook" or "disregard," as
in Philippians 3:13, "forgetting what lies behind." Perhaps a
sense like "modestly dismissed" better fits the logic of the story.

## CHAPTER 12

1. Mary made the purple and scarlet and brought them to the priest, and he blessed her and said, "O Mary, the Lord God has magnified your name, and you shall be blessed in all the generations of the earth."

2. And Mary rejoiced and went away to her kinswoman Elizabeth and knocked at her door. When Elizabeth heard this, she threw down the scarlet thread she was working and ran to the door and opened it.[40] And when she saw Mary she blessed her and said, "Whence is this to me, that the mother of my Lord should come to me? Look how the child in me leaps and blesses you!"[41] But Mary had forgotten[42] the mysteries that were told her by the Archangel Gabriel. Looking up into heaven she said, "Who am I, Lord, that all generations should call me blessed?"

3. She remained three months with Elizabeth, and day by day her womb grew. And Mary was afraid, and went into her own house and hid herself from the children of Israel. She was sixteen years old when these mysteries occurred.

43 It is six months after the Annunciation, and Joseph has been away long enough for the difference in Mary's form to be visible. Another September has come, and the infant John is three months old.

44 An element of Mary's tradition holds that she did not try to explain or justify her condition. Instead she "kept all these things, pondering them in her heart" (Lk. 2:19), keeping private her experience of a mystery that is fundamentally inexpressible.

## CHAPTER 13

1. Now when she was in her sixth month, behold, Joseph returned[43] from building his houses. He came into his house and found Mary big with child. He struck himself on the face, and threw himself on the ground in sackcloth, crying out, "How can I lift up my face to the Lord God? What prayer can I make about this girl? I received her as a virgin from the temple of the Lord, and I have not protected her. Who has deceived me? Who did this evil in my house, and defiled the virgin? Is not the history of Adam repeated in me? In the very hour of his glory, the serpent came and found Eve alone—the same has happened to me."

2. Rising up from his sackcloth Joseph called Mary and said to her, "You were cared for by God; why have you done this? Why have you humiliated your soul? Have you forgotten the Lord your God, you who were nurtured in the Holy of Holies, and received food from the hand of an angel?"

3. But Mary wept bitterly and said, "As the Lord God lives, I am pure! I have never known a man!" Joseph said to her, "Then whence is this in your womb?" And she said, "As the Lord my God lives, I do not understand how this came to my womb."[44]

45 The Law of Moses, recorded in the book of Leviticus, instructs that a man or woman who commits adultery must be put to death. Concealing Mary's pregnancy could make Joseph party to a crime. Yet, in St. Matthew's words, he is "a just man and unwilling to put her to shame" (Mt. 1:19). He also considers it at least a possibility that something "angelic" is taking place. With these conflicting and troubled thoughts, Joseph falls asleep.

## CHAPTER 14

1. At this Joseph was greatly afraid. He parted from her, wondering what he should do with her. And Joseph said, "If I conceal her sin, I shall be found rebelling against the law of the Lord.[45] But if I expose her to the children of Israel, I am afraid; perhaps what is in her is angelic, and I shall be found betraying innocent blood to the judgment of death. What then shall I do? I will send her away from me secretly." And while he was pondering these things, night overtook him.

2. And, behold, an angel of the Lord appeared to him in a dream, saying: "Joseph son of David, do not fear this child, for that begotten in her is of the Holy Spirit. You will call his name Jesus, for he will save the people from their sins." Rising up from sleep, Joseph glorified the God of Israel who had given him this grace, and he protected the girl.

46 Annas has dropped in at Joseph's house, wondering why he
did not come to worship as soon as he returned from his trip.
Something urgent had occupied Joseph's attention from his
arrival until nightfall. Mary has concealed her pregnancy up till
now by staying in the house, but as she fulfills the duty of a
hostess, her guest can't help noting her condition.

## CHAPTER 15

1. Now Annas the scribe came to him[46] and said, "Why have you not appeared at our assembly?" And Joseph replied, "I was weary from the road, and rested for one day." Then Annas, turning away, saw that the virgin was big with child.

2. He went running to the priest and told him, "Joseph, whom you vouched for, has sinned grievously." And the priest said, "How so?" And Annas replied, "He has defiled the virgin whom he received from the temple of the Lord, and secretly taken her as his wife, without revealing it to the children of Israel." And answering, the high priest said to him, "Has Joseph done this?" And Annas said, "Send officers, and you will find the virgin big with child." And the officers went and found her just as he had said, and they brought her and Joseph to the court.

3. And the priest said, "Mary, why have you done these things? Why have you humiliated your soul, and forgotten the Lord your God? You were nurtured in the Holy of Holies and received food from the hand an angel; you heard their hymns and danced before the Lord. Why have you done this?" But she wept bitterly, saying, "As the Lord God lives, I am pure before Him, and have not known a man."

47 "Humble yourselves therefore under the mighty hand of God" (1 Pet. 5:6).

48 It would have been permissible for Joseph and Mary to have children, after a public ceremony finalizing their marital relationship. The priest charges that instead (in the Greek idiom) they have "stolen" their wedding.

49 Numbers 5:11–31 explains that if a "spirit of jealousy" prompts a man to think his wife has cheated on him, he is to bring her to the temple, where the priest will give her a drink of water mixed with dust from the tabernacle floor. If she collapses in agonizing pain, she's guilty; if she remains unharmed, she's innocent. This simple test may have freed many a woman from the accusations of a jealous husband.

50 "It will make your sin apparent to your eyes." The high priest does not administer the test to prove their guilt, but to assist them in recognizing their own sin.

4. The priest said, "Joseph, why have you done this?" And Joseph answered, "As the Lord my God lives, I am faultless concerning her." The priest said, "Now do not lie, but tell the truth. You have married her by stealth, and did not reveal it to the children of Israel. You did not bow your head beneath the mighty hand of God,[47] so that your offspring would be blessed."[48] And Joseph was silent.

## CHAPTER 16

1. Then the priest told him, "Now give back the virgin whom you received from the temple of the Lord." And Joseph began to weep. The priest said, "I will give you the water of the Lord's rebuke to drink,[49] and it will make your sin apparent to your eyes."[50]

2. And the priest took it and gave it to Joseph to drink, then sent him out into hill-country; and Joseph returned unharmed. Then he gave it to the virgin to drink and sent her out into the hill-country; and she returned unharmed. And all the people were amazed that sin was not found in them.

3. So the priest said, "If the Lord God does not reveal your sin, then neither will I condemn you." And Joseph took Mary and went to his house, rejoicing and glorifying the God of Israel.

51 Luke tells us: "In those days a decree went out from Caesar Augustus that all the world should be enrolled."

52 This is a well-loved line from Psalm 118: "This is the day which the LORD has made."

53 The two peoples have been traditionally understood as two branches of the Jewish people: those who rejected Jesus, and those who accepted him. The latter include those Gentiles who believed in Jesus through their preaching, and are "grafted into . . .the olive tree" of Israel, as St. Paul explains in his letter to the Romans.

54 My Greek dictionary says that *shame* is a euphemism for "private parts" (which is also a euphemism). The story is not coy about the process of childbirth.

## CHAPTER 17

1. There went out a command from Augustus the King to register everyone in Bethlehem of Judea.[51] Joseph said, "I will register my sons, but what shall I do about this girl? How shall she be registered? As my wife? I am ashamed. Perhaps as my daughter? But all the children of Israel know that she is not my daughter. This is the day the Lord has made;[52] it will turn out as he wills."

2. So he saddled his donkey and set her upon it, and his son led it while Joseph followed. As they came to the third mile, Joseph turned and saw that she looked sad. He said to himself, "Perhaps that which is within her is causing her pain." But the next time Joseph turned he saw her laughing, and he said, "Mary, how is it with you? For I see your face at one time happy, and at another it is sad." And she said to him, "Joseph, my eyes behold two peoples: one afflicted and grieving, and one joyful and exulting."[53]

3. When they came to the middle of the journey, Mary said to him, "Help me down from the donkey, for that which is within me presses me to come forth." And he took her down, then said, "Where shall I take you, to cover your shame?[54] For this is a desert place."

55 Those familiar with the usual Christmas story are wondering: Where's the stable? In Israel, where wood is scarce, it is unlikely that livestock would be housed in a wooden structure; instead, animals would be kept in any available cave. That's the case here; later Mary will place her child in a manger. Hymns and icons of the Eastern Church have always depicted the Nativity of Christ as taking place in a cave, and the swaddled child against the cave's black mouth intentionally suggests a shrouded body in a tomb.

Our cultural tradition has embroidered the Christmas story with many elements not mentioned in the Scriptures. St. Luke's Gospel tells us that Mary placed the child in a manger, but doesn't describe the setting. Christmas tales describe the couple being turned away from an inn, but the Gospel tells us only that there was no room in the inn; it doesn't say that Joseph spoke to an innkeeper, or that the birthplace was near an inn.

56 In his treatise against Helvidius, AD 383, Jerome insisted that "no midwife assisted at [Jesus'] birth" because "with her own hands [Mary] wrapped him in the swaddling clothes" (see Luke 2:7). That Scripture, he claims, "refutes the ravings of the apocryphal accounts [*deliramenta apocryphorum*]." This Gospel may escape his censure on a technicality, because the midwife is present only as a witness.

57 There is no explanation for why the story goes to the first person here, though it's certainly a dramatic effect, if you picture it being told to an audience of rapt listeners. Just as Christ's birth is heralded here by the astonishment of all earthly life, his death will be marked by earthquakes, darkness, and the rending of the temple veil (Mt. 27:45, 51–53).

Earlier scholars thought that the change of voice, and other variations throughout, might indicate that the Gospel originated as several different documents. The discovery of a fourth-century fragment that runs from chapters 13 through 23 demonstrates instead early unity.

## CHAPTER 18

1. So he found a cave there and settled her in it,[55] and set his sons to care for her, and then went out to find a Hebrew midwife[56] in the neighborhood of Bethlehem.

2. "Then I, Joseph,[57] was walking, but somehow I did not walk. I looked up to the vault of the heavens, and saw it standing still, and into the air and saw it astonished, and the birds of the heavens motionless. And I looked upon the earth and saw a platter resting, and workmen reclining, and their hands were in the dish. But the ones who were chewing did not chew, and the ones reaching did not reach, and the ones carrying food to their mouths did not carry it; but all their faces were looking upward.

3. "And I saw sheep being driven, yet the sheep stood still; and the shepherd raised his hand to strike them with his staff, and his hand remained up. And I looked upon the water-brook and I saw the kids put their mouths down upon  the water and not drink. And suddenly all things moved forward in their course."

58 "Yes, *kyria*," the feminine form of *Kyrie*, Lord.

59 A "bright cloud" overshadowed the disciples when they saw
   Jesus transfigured on the mountain (Mt. 17:5), and a glorious
   cloud filled Moses' tent of meeting (Ex. 40:34) and Solomon's
   temple (1 Kings 8:10–11).

60 The mode of the birth is not described, but even at this early
   date a belief is circulating that it did not compromise Mary's
   physical virginity. It seems strange to us that this was so
   important to the early Christians. In trying to understand
   them, we can remember that childbirth took place in a much
   less private setting than it does today. People could not avoid
   having an earthy, graphic familiarity with the process, and
   would understand what a claim of post-birth virginity meant:
   a miracle. To them, this would be one more sign of God's
   miraculous intervention in Christ's birth.

## CHAPTER 19

1. "And, behold, a woman was coming down from the hill-country, and she said to me, 'Man, where are you going?' And I said to her, 'I seek a Hebrew midwife.'
And answering me she said, 'Are you from Israel?'
And I said to her, 'Yes, Lady.'[58]
And she said to me, 'Who is it that gives birth in the cave?'
And I said, 'My betrothed.'
And she said to me, 'She is not your wife?'
And I said to her, 'It is Mary who was brought up in the temple of the Lord; I received her by lot as my wife, but she is not my wife, and she has conceived by the Holy Spirit.'"
And the midwife said to him, "Is this true?"
And he said to her, "Come and see." And she went with him.

2. And they stood at the place of the cave, and a bright cloud[59] overshadowed the cave. And the midwife said, "My soul is magnified this day, for my eyes have seen marvelous things; salvation has been born to Israel!" And immediately the cloud drew back from the cave, and a light shone so brightly in the cave that our eyes could not bear it. And in a little while that light drew back until the baby was revealed; and he came and took the breast of his mother, Mary.[60] And the midwife cried out, "This day is great for me, because today I have seen this new sight."

61 Apparently Salome is another midwife. The fact that she
enters the story named but not identified suggests that the
audience would already know her. Perhaps this is the Salome
who later became one of Jesus' followers, who stood at the
cross with the Virgin and Mary Magdalene, and who was one
of the "myrrh-bearing women" who brought spices to the
tomb.

62 "Physical condition" tries to render *physis*, a broad term
covering the nature or natural condition of something, the natural order, species, or kind (from it we get "physical"). The
*physis* of women does not allow for virginity after childbirth.
Salome vows to test Mary's *physis*.

63 Thomas uses nearly identical phrasing in John 20:25, "Unless
I . . . place my hand in his side, I will not believe."

3. And the midwife went out of the cave and met Salome,[61] and said to her, "Salome, Salome, I must tell you of a new sight! A virgin has given birth, a thing which the physical condition[62] of women does not allow!"

And Salome said, "As the Lord God lives, unless I place my finger and test her physical condition,[63] I will not believe that a virgin has given birth."

64 The Greek text echoes a line in the Septuagint, a Greek translation of the Hebrew Scriptures that was commonly used in Jesus' time (it is the source of most Scriptural citations in the New Testament). In that translation, Isaiah 7:13 reads: "Is it a small thing to you to have a contention with men? How is it you have a contention with God as well?" The next verse memorably continues: "Therefore the Lord himself will give you a sign: a virgin will conceive. . . ."

65 The story that Mary was examined by a midwife after birth, and found to be still virgin, circulated among the early Christians; it's mentioned by Clement of Alexandria, in his *Stromata* (AD 202).

66 "You shall not put the LORD your God to the test" (Deut. 6:16; quoted by Jesus in Mt. 4:7).

CHAPTER 20

1. And the midwife went in and said, "Mary, get yourself ready, for no small contention[64] has arisen concerning you." And Salome placed her finger to test her physical condition.[65] And Salome cried out saying, "Woe for my lawlessness and woe for my faithlessness! For I have tested[66] the living God, and look, my hand is burning off in flames!"

2. And Salome dropped to her knees before the Lord, saying, "O God of my fathers, remember me, for I am the child of Abraham and Isaac and Jacob; do not make me a mockery to the children of Israel, but restore me to the poor. For you know, Lord, that in your name I have performed my services, and received payment only from you."

3. And suddenly an angel of the Lord stood before Salome saying, "Salome, Salome, the Lord God has listened to your prayer. Stretch out your hand to the child and hold him, and he will be to you salvation and joy."

4. And Salome came and held him, and she said, "I worship him, for a great king has been born to Israel." And immediately Salome was healed, and went out from the cave having been made righteous. And there came a loud voice saying, "Salome, Salome, do not tell of the strange wonders you have seen until the child comes into Jerusalem."

67 Bethlehem is *in* Judea, of course, as is noted in the following phrase. Joseph is preparing to go out of Bethlehem and into the surrounding countryside, as he begins his journey home. He and his family will thus providentially escape the "great uproar" that is about to engulf Bethlehem, when Herod responds to the Magi's visit by taking drastic action against the threat of an infant rival.

68 This story is also told in Matthew 2:1–12.

## CHAPTER 21

1. And, behold, Joseph was preparing to go out into Judea,[67] and a great uproar was about to take place in Bethlehem of Judea. For Magi had come from the east saying, "Where is the one born king of the Jews? For we have seen his star in the east and have come to worship him."

2. And hearing this Herod was troubled, and he sent officers to the Magi. He also sent for the high priests and questioned them, saying, "How is it written of the Christ? Where is he to be born?" They said, "In Bethlehem of Judea, for thus it is written." He released them, and questioned the Magi, saying to them, "What sign did you see concerning the one born a king?" And the Magi said, "We saw a very great star shining among these stars, and dimming them so that their light no longer shone. By this we knew that a king has been born to Israel, and we have come to worship him." And Herod said, "Go and seek for him, and when you have found him tell me, so I too may come and worship him."

3. And the Magi went out, and the star that they had beheld in the east led them until they came to the cave, where it stopped over the head of the child. And seeing him with his mother Mary, the Magi worshiped him, and opening their treasures gave him gold and frankincense and myrrh. And having been warned by a holy angel not to go back into Judea, they returned to their land by another route.[68]

69 "Then Herod, when he saw that he had been tricked by the
[Magi] . . . sent and killed all the male children in Bethlehem
and in all that region who were two years old or under" (Mt.
2:16).

70 Luke tells us, "And she . . . laid him in a manger." It seems
here that Mary conceals Jesus temporarily in a manger.

71 It is now late December or early January, and the infant John
is six months old. Herod is seeking John in particular, because
the unusual circumstances surrounding his conception and
birth would have aroused Herod's suspicions.

72 The mountain became, in Greek, "diaphanous." The tradition
holds that Elizabeth lived there with John for the rest of her
life. When John was grown he came out of the wilderness as
a powerful preacher. "John the baptizer appeared in the
wilderness, preaching a baptism of repentance for the forgiveness
of sins" (Mk. 1:4).

## CHAPTER 22

1. When Herod knew that he had been tricked by the Magi, he was enraged, and sent assassins and commanded them to kill the children who were two years old and younger.[69]

2. When Mary heard that the children were being killed, she was afraid; she took the child and swaddled him, and laid him in an ox-manger.[70]

3. And Elizabeth, when she heard that they were seeking John,[71] took him and went up into the hill-country. She looked around for a place she might hide him, but there was no hiding place. Then Elizabeth groaned and said in a loud voice, "O mountain of God, receive a mother and her child," for she was unable to climb any higher. And immediately the mountain split open and received them. And that mountain became translucent[72] to them, and an angel of the Lord was with them and protected them.

73 In Matthew 23:35, Jesus warns, ". . . that upon you may come all the righteous blood shed on earth, from the blood of innocent Abel to the blood of Zachariah the son of Barachiah, whom you murdered between the sanctuary and the altar." Zechariah (Greek, Zacharias) was a popular name, and it is hard to tell who was meant. In 2 Chronicles 24:21 we read of a Zechariah who was stoned to death "in the court of the house of the LORD," circa 790 BC, but his father's name was Jehoida. The prophet Zechariah, about 520 BC, tells us he is the son of Berechiah (Zech. 1:1), but he was not killed in the temple. Neither fit this saying of Jesus, but perhaps this Zacharias does.

## CHAPTER 23

1. But Herod was seeking the infant John, and sent officers to the altar of the Lord, to say to Zacharias, "Where have you hidden your son?" And he said to them, "I am here as a minister of the Lord God, serving in his temple; I do not know where my son is."

2. The officers came and reported this to Herod. And Herod was enraged and said, "His son is to be king over Israel." And he sent unto Zacharias again, saying, "Tell me the truth! Where is your son? Know this: your blood is under my hand." The officers departed and told him these things.

3. And Zacharias said, "I am a martyr of God if my blood is spilled, for the Lord will receive my spirit; but you shed innocent blood at the entrance of the temple of the Lord."[73] At about daybreak Zacharias was slain. And the children of Israel did not know that he was slain.

74 They waited for Zacharias similarly on the day he saw the angel and heard the prophecy of John's birth: "And the people were waiting for Zechariah, and they wondered at his delay in the temple" (Lk. 1:21).

75 In the Septuagint, Amos 8:3 reads: "And the ceiling panels of the temple shall wail in that day."

76 This is the Simeon who greeted Mary and Joseph when they came to present the infant Jesus in the temple, and who sang, "Lord, now lettest thou thy servant depart in peace, according to thy word" (see Lk. 2:25–35).

## CHAPTER 24

1. At the hour of greeting the priests were departing, and Zacharias did not bless them as usual. So the priests stood waiting for Zacharias,[74] to greet him with prayer and to glorify the Most High.

2. But as he delayed to come they all became afraid. One of them took courage and entered in, and beside the altar of the Lord he saw congealed blood. And then a voice said: "Zacharias has been murdered, and his blood shall not be wiped away until his avenger comes." Hearing this word he was frightened, and went and told the high priests what he had heard and seen.

3. And they all took courage and went in and saw what had happened. From the ceiling panels of the temple there came the sound of wailing,[75] and the priests rent their clothing from top to bottom. The body of Zacharias they did not find, but they found his blood, turned hard as stone. And they were afraid, and went out and told all the people that Zacharias had been murdered. And hearing this, all the tribes of the people mourned for three days and three nights.

4. And after the three days, the priests took counsel as to who they should appoint in his stead, and the lot fell upon Simeon.[76] Now he was the one to whom it had been revealed by the Holy Spirit that he would not see death, until he had seen Christ in the flesh.

77 This seems to mean that James wrote the work while he was
in the desert, away from the discord that arose in Jerusalem
following Herod's death in AD 4. If it's hard to believe that St.
James wrote this gospel, it's even more of a stretch to believe
that he wrote it while Jesus was still a little child. The early
Christians apparently shared our skepticism, and while they
regarded the Epistle of James as coming authentically from the
pen of the Lord's brother, and included it in the canon of
Scripture, they did not offer this gospel the same honor.

   Nevertheless, they found this gospel intriguing, appealing,
and useful as an aid to devotion. We may agree with them
there, too.

## Chapter 25

1. Now I, James, wrote this history when an uproar arose upon Herod's death in Jerusalem, and took myself into the desert until the uproar had ceased.[77] I glorify God, who gave me the gift and the wisdom to write this history. Grace will rest on all who fear our Lord Jesus Christ, to whom be glory for ever and ever. Amen.

# TWO

# Asking
# Mary's Prayers

*Compassion*

IN 1917, THE JOHN RYLANDS UNIVERSITY LIBRARY in Manchester, England, purchased a torn scrap of papyrus that had been uncovered in Egypt. It was a small item, the tattered remains of a rectangle about the size of an index card. The message on it, just ten lines long, didn't look like a carefully inscribed passage from a book, but rather like something jotted down for personal reference. It bore a couple of hasty misspellings, such as "im" for "in."

The fabric of the papyrus was gouged and nibbled, and the first letter was gone, but the opening words were tantalizing: ". . . nder . . . compassion. . . ." The real shocker, though, came at the fourth line. It clearly read "Theotoke." That "e" on the end is the form used when you're speaking to someone. These lines were addressed to the Theotokos—that is, the Birthgiver of God.

*When did Christians begin to pray to Mary? And why?*

In the previous text, the *Gospel of Mary*, we saw the character of their love for her: they doted on her, with the protectiveness we instinctively feel toward a sweet-natured, innocent girl. This tenderness is evident in a fresco painting of the Virgin Mary that appears in one of the chambers of the Roman catacomb named for St. Priscilla. It is the earliest existing image of Mary, dating to around AD 225.

Mary is seated with her infant son on her lap, and this image is still unfamiliar enough that the artist has set a prophet on the left, who points to a star over Mary's head for clarification. Both mother and child are turning to look at us, as if our walking up has prompted them to take a break from breastfeeding. Despite erosion and damage to the red-ocher image, the gentle, lively natural-ism of the pair speaks across the centuries. People in all times and places have found the sight of a loving mother and child delightful, cheering, comforting. The variations on this theme are so promising that it will recur throughout the history of Christian art, and become the most common way of depicting the Virgin.

But elsewhere in this same catacomb there is a slightly later image that expands our understanding of how the early Christians saw Mary. In this fresco she is praying. She is standing with her hands lifted, in the traditional posture called the *orans* (praying) position. She is facing us directly, and her eyes are arresting. In this image Mary is clearly a warrior of prayer, and is challenging us to pray alongside her.

(Her Child is also present, facing us frontally and positioned directly in front of her chest. This might seem improbable since, with her hands in the air, she can't be holding him up. Future variations on this image will enclose him in an oval disk, that is, her womb; this image of the pregnant Virgin is called "The Virgin of the Sign," after the prophecy in Isaiah 7:14: "The Lord himself will give you a sign; behold, a virgin shall conceive and bear a son . . ." [LXX]. You'll frequently find the Virgin of the Sign filling the apse behind the altar in Eastern Orthodox churches.)

### *How old?*

When the eminent papyrologist Edward Lobel examined the papyrus (soon catalogued as "Papyrus Rylands 470"), he recognized the handwriting style as characteristic of the mid-third century—around AD 250, the same general date as the catacomb fresco of Mary at prayer. But Colin Roberts, who edited a collection of Rylands papyri published in 1938, could not bring himself to agree. He found it "almost incredible that a prayer addressed so directly to the Virgin in these terms could be written in the third century." He recommended a date a century later instead. He offered a reconstruction of the prayer as well, based on his best guess at the missing words.

That guess was not accurate, however. It was not until 1994 that the prayer on this papyrus was correctly identified. James Shiel, a professor at the University of Sussex, was leafing through the decades-old Roberts volume when he came across a reproduction of the papyrus. He recognized in it a phrase that occurs in the well-loved Latin prayer *Sub tuum praesidium* (a phrase present in the *Memorare* as well). But these prayers had always been considered products of the medieval era. The earliest written examples were from the fourteenth century.

With more investigation, Shiel discovered that the prayer also appears in the Greek Orthodox "Book of Hours," the cycle of daily prayers; it is still among the concluding prayers of the evening services. Shiel found that the Greek prayer in current use—in use, apparently, for 1,750 years—supplied perfectly the letters torn away from the papyrus:

Under your
compassion
we take refuge,
Theotokos; do not
overlook our prayers
in the midst of tribulation,
but deliver us
from danger,
O only pure,
only blessed one.

Long years ago a Christian heard this prayer and wrote it down on a piece of papyrus that was small enough to carry through the day—the earliest prayer yet found that is addressed to Mary. As Shiel says, "Such things were part of an oral tradition. If they ever got written down it was rather by some act of individual devotion." The date of AD 250 tells us only when it was inscribed on this particular papyrus. We don't know how far back the prayer itself might go.

This prayer begins with Mary's compassion. It does not speak of taking refuge under her power or her merits, but instead cites a motivation inside of her: she loves us. A person moved by love is a sure help in trouble, and will pour out what could not be won by bargaining or flattery. A child knows this about his mother, that her love is something strong, and is a good place to find shelter.

This prayer sends pleas to Mary from "the midst of tribulation," the tossing sea of life. It asks, "deliver us from danger," using the same verb for "deliver" that is found in the Lord's Prayer. It is sobering to recall that this prayer was first used by Christians who lived while their faith was still a capital crime, and for them "deliver us from danger" might have been an urgent appeal.

What shall we make of "only pure, only blessed one"? Certainly, Jesus was also pure? And aren't we all blessed? There is a tendency in Eastern Christianity to engage in affectionate overstatement. This is poetry, not an engineering manual, and more like the kind of thing little children say to their mothers than like later academic theology.

We can discern a shift here from the earlier text. In the *Gospel of Mary*, the Virgin is a tender figure who deserves protection. Now she is a champion of prayer, and we rely on her compassion to protect us.

Two things are shocking about this. First is the expectation that Mary is still alive, and able to hear such a request. In his commentary on the Gospel of Luke, John Calvin verbalized something that has no doubt occurred to many: when Christians adopt the angel's greeting, "Hail Mary," they "salute someone who is absent." But here we see that the early Christians believed she *was* there. They believed this because of what they believed about death—and what comes after death.

The second shocking thing is the expectation that Mary's prayers are effective. That wouldn't be true only of Mary, of course; any member of the company of the departed saints could be a strong intercessor. It seems that asking for the prayers of saints was a widespread personal impulse, not something done only during formal, corporate prayer. In the Roman catacomb named for St. Sebastian, where the bones of St. Paul and St. Peter were placed around AD 250, the names of those saints and requests for their prayers were scratched on the walls over a hundred times. The early Christians believed that it is right and good to pray to Mary and other saints, and they also believed that it was effective. As the old slogan says, "Prayer changes things."

### Victory Over Death

Let's begin with the first item and explore how early Christians looked at death. Stop anybody on the street and ask for a one-sentence definition of Christianity, and you're apt to hear something along these lines: "Jesus died on the cross to pay for our sins." But it doesn't take much reading in the works of the early Christians to realize that they were focused on something beyond that which resulted from the Cross and Resurrection. The empty tomb means something for all of us. Christ's victory has rescued us from death.

We should probably give that a capital D, for we find New Testament and later writers treating Death almost as a personification of the malice of the Evil One. The letter to the Hebrews explains that the Evil One has always kept the human race in bondage through our fear of death. Jesus took on our human form so that he could go into death, so that "through death he might destroy him who has the power of death, that is, the devil" (Heb. 2:14). St. Paul explains that when Jesus nailed our debt to the cross, he "disarmed the principalities and powers," mocking them publicly and triumphing over them (Col. 2:14–15). The demonic claim on our souls and our imprisonment in death as the fitting wage of sin were overthrown.

St. Paul cites the prophet Isaiah's prediction that one day Death would be swallowed up forever (Is. 25:8). He then ridicules this fallen enemy: "O Death, where is thy victory? O Death, where is thy sting?"(1 Cor. 15:54).

We don't feel as shadowed by Death's hovering presence as our forebears did. Now we scarcely begrudge Death, reasoning that "everybody's gotta go sometime." And Death reciprocates, as a rule, behaving circumspectly and waiting to harvest those who have completed a long life, often doing so in sterile, private settings. For these and other reasons Death is not as brutally present as it once was.

There are tragic exceptions to that general rule, as my family and every other family knows. But these tragedies are in part so shocking because they are so unexpected.

In centuries past Death was everywhere, wild and profligate, snatching away children in kitchen fires, young men in hunting accidents, babies and mothers together in childbed. A broken limb, badly set, could lead to the grave. A fever could steal overnight, not just one child, but all the children in a home. The cities were impossibly crowded—ancient Antioch housed more people per acre than Manhattan, yet without modern high-rises—and correspondingly filled with crime, vermin, and disease. Buildings were prone to collapse, and fires leapt from one rickety structure to the next. Cities were also unimaginably filthy. The single most important element in extending human life on earth is improved sanitation.

Today researchers give American newborns a life expectancy nearing 80, and predict that half of them will see their nineties. But throughout most of human history, a newborn's life expectancy ranged between 20 and 30 years. (This doesn't mean, by the way, that a person was elderly at 25. An uninterrupted life would still extend naturally to 70 or 80 years, as Psalm 90:10 notes. But so many lives were interrupted that the average was driven down.)

Virtually every family buried some of their children. As recently as 1850, Harriet Beecher Stowe could evoke sympathy for Uncle Tom's tears at being torn from his children by reminding readers that they had shed similar tears "into the coffin where lay your first-born son" and "when you heard the cries of your dying babe." Not if, but when.

At the time Christ came, Death lingered close at every elbow. Everyone had lost many whom they depended on and cherished. This is why the most stirring claim about Christ's work was that Death had been vanquished. When Christ was crucified, he went into the realm of Death and destroyed its power, then rose to life again. With himself he freed all those who were held captive, like the freeing of the Hebrews from slavery in Egypt. The Greek biblical word for salvation, *soteria*, captures this sense: it means rescued from danger, freed from slavery, restored to freedom, "saved" as in "saved from drowning."

This was astoundingly good news. Death, once fearsome, was now proved a puny weakling. Christians' contempt of death was so well-known in the Roman Empire that St. Athanasius could use it as proof of Christ's Resurrection. In his treatise "On the Incarnation" (around AD 320), he wrote, "Before the divine sojourn of the Savior, even the holiest of men were afraid of death, and mourned the dead as those who perish. But now that the Savior has raised His body, death is no longer terrible, but all those who believe in Christ tread it underfoot as nothing."

### *"The prayers of the saints"*

Particularly when they were gathered for worship, the living were aware that they stood together with the departed who are alive in Christ. The ones who had been mourned, the golden child and the young husband, were then invisibly present among the "great cloud of witnesses" (Heb. 12:1). Worship raised the whole earthly community into the heavenly throne room, where it joined with the elders as they sing their ceaseless praise, in the presence of the angels lifting bowls of incense, "which are the prayers of the saints" (Rev. 5:8).

The departed, present in spirit, were sometimes literally present in body as well: altars were built over the tombs of saints, and saints' bones were placed inside altars. The bodies of the holy dead were not garbage to be burned, but the worthy remains of a vessel of the Holy Spirit. In the Book of Revelation, St. John hears the voice of those slain for Christ crying out from "beneath the altar." Roman Catholic and Eastern Orthodox churches still continue this custom of interring saints' bones within consecrated altars.

If departed family members are alive in Christ, so also are the Apostles and martyrs, and the holy prophets who yearned for his appearing. The entire heavenly court mingled invisibly with earthly worshipers. Borrowing the Roman custom of decorating walls with frescoes and mosaics of heroic figures, Christians covered the interiors of their churches with portraits of departed saints. To a worshiper, it looked as if St. Andrew the Apostle and St. Thecla the evangelist were standing next to Joseph the baker and Miriam the weaver—as indeed they were.

If death has truly been destroyed, then these departed friends in Christ are alive and invisibly present; they are just as genuinely present as the friends and family we can see. But now they are also in the throne room of God, and continually at prayer. The early Christians had such complete confidence that death had been overthrown, that they asked the holy departed to pray for them.

## Why?

An obvious question at this point is "Why?" Why not just go directly to the Lord? Why fool around with intermediaries?

Of course, Christians did continue to go directly to the Lord. Enlisting the prayers of the saints did not replace that; they weren't thought to stand *between* the Christian and his Lord, like gatekeepers. Their prayers were supportive, supplementary, much as we ask friends to add their prayers to ours when we have a special need.

After all, we don't meet the saints or anybody else—or, for that matter, do or say or even think *anything*—outside the presence of Christ. Christ is "everywhere present and filling all things," as an ancient prayer says about the Holy Spirit.

So you could picture this being like standing with a circle of friends in general conversation at a party, and then addressing a comment or question to one particular member of the group. When you ask an earthly or heavenly friend, living or departed, to join you in prayer, it's like asking a question of one member of a discussion circle, or enlisting him in your support, saying, "Help me out here."

But the more you think about the whole matter of intercessory prayer, the more puzzling it gets. Why ask anybody, even a friend, to pray for you? Why do you need help? Can't you take care of it directly?

In fact, why pray at all? Isn't God going to have his will anyway, one way or another?

And yet it is undeniable that God wants us to pray, for ourselves and for each other. Jesus' parable of the widow and the unrighteous judge calls us to vigorous, persistent prayer (Lk. 18:1–7). God wants us to be whole-hearted participants in his work, though he obviously doesn't need our help to do anything.

Perhaps this is like a mom having her children help her make cookies, though she could do it a lot more efficiently alone. God loves us. He wants us to participate in his work, because he wants to be in communion with us. The whole universe is arranged for the very purpose of enabling creatures to encounter God.

And since God is Love, love should be our prime occupation. Everything else will fade. Even if we achieved world-wide justice and perfect peace, it wouldn't last. The only thing that lasts is love, because love is an element of God's very being.

There's a mystery about the *dynamics* of all this, too. God is Life, too, so being with and in him means doing something active: praying, working, cooperating. The holy departed take part in this work as well. They don't just wait in suspended animation until the Last Trump blows: "He is not God of the dead, but of the living," Jesus said.

St. Paul uses the concept of synergy. He told the Corinthians, "We are God's *synergoi*," fellow-workers cooperating in a dynamic, unfolding story. And those who join together in prayer begin to be affected by prayer in turn. As they draw near God, they begin to understand more clearly where he is leading and how to cooperate with him. Sometimes they discover that he is leading in a wholly unexpected direction. "Prayer changes things," and often the first thing that changes is us.

So when you ask earthly or heavenly friends to pray, you're not asking them to make the request happen by their own magic powers. You're asking them to join you as *synergoi* in this mysterious thing, the will and work of God. And, somehow, that participation sets dynamic forces in motion.

Intercessory prayer has easily recognizable, practical effects: it opens us to hear God's will, prepares us to recognize his work, and knits us together with other believers everywhere. Saintly prayer-companions don't replace Christ, but enhance our worship, just as the presence of friends makes a festive meal more joyous.

## Faces in the Cloud

But you can see your earthly prayer partner, and you can't see the Virgin Mary or any of the other saints in the "great cloud of witnesses" (Heb. 12:1). It seems a bit like throwing postcards into a canyon, to make requests of the holy departed who, no matter how heroic, are also impalpable, inaudible, and invisible. How can we "know" them?

Not through a séance or anything like that. The book of Leviticus makes it plain that God's people are not to use mediums or wizards to seek guidance for the future. In a dramatic story in the 1 Samuel 28, King Saul is so desperate that he hires a medium to call up the ghost of the prophet Samuel. He gets only a harsh rebuke for his trouble. We are supposed to trust the Lord's providence for our future, and not try to get around it by seeking advice from the dead.

A better way of looking at the presence of the holy departed is found in the story of Christ's Transfiguration. When Peter, James, and John were on the mountaintop with Jesus, they had a momentary glimpse into heavenly realities. Jesus was transfigured before them, and became more radiant than the sun. Elijah and Moses appeared beside him, talking to him. (And don't you wonder what they talked about!) Some kind of loving melody, or exchange, or conversation is going on eternally in heaven, among the holy departed and the angelic host and the undivided Trinity. For a brief moment, these three Apostles glimpsed it.

Some Christians who have found prayer companions among the saints report that it has enhanced their faith in undeniable ways—prayers answered, miracles attained, peace received. Sometimes a person discovers a connection with a saint who bore the same name. Sometimes a person keeps running into quotations from and references to a particular saint, and finds they are consistently relevant; gradually he gets the feeling that a link is being formed.

Though all saints are loved in their home community—the saying about "prophets without honor" reversed—certain saints were held particularly dear everywhere Christianity spread. Sometimes we can identify a reason: St. Peter and St. Paul are obvious examples, along with other Apostles and saints honored for their heroic roles in the Bible story.

But some post-biblical saints were also embraced enthusiastically, all around the world, for reasons that are not immediately clear. What made St. Nicholas of Myra stand out, among all the saintly bishops in fourth-century Asia Minor? He may be the most popular non-biblical saint (though in our land his memory has been distorted into Santa Claus). Or perhaps St. George would take that title. This Palestinian knight was martyred in AD 304, and has been claimed as patron not only in Palestine but also in Ethiopia, Canada, Slovenia, England, Germany, Lithuania, Greece, Sicily, Portugal, Moscow, and Beirut. Why him, among all the courageous saints?

Perhaps believers who regularly call on the same saint experience something similar to the effect biographers sometimes report, that after long immersion in study of a subject's life, they began inexplicably to feel the person present with them. Occasionally you hear stories of a more startlingly overt presence—a biographer might report apprehending a message from the work's subject in a dream, for example—but usually it's vaguer than that, something that can't be adequately described, but it sure isn't nothing.

It's not unusual to hear stories like this about encounters with the presence of the Lord. A typical example is the experience of the late Russian Orthodox bishop,

Metropolitan Anthony Bloom. As a teen he was hostile to Christianity, and having heard a talk that presented Christ in a foolish, sentimental way, he resolved to read the Gospel and confirm that Jesus was indeed a ninny.

What happened next was a story the bishop would retell for the rest of his life. As he turned the pages of St. Mark's Gospel, he said, he became aware of a presence standing on the other side of his desk. Even when he raised his eyes to stare at the spot, the powerful presence never wavered, though nothing could be heard or seen.

At that moment Metropolitan Anthony concluded that "if Christ is standing here alive, that means he is the risen Christ. . . . I know from my own personal experience that Christ is risen and that therefore everything that is said about him in the Gospel is true."

If Christ's victory over Death means that he is alive and permeating this world, then the "great cloud" of saints is similarly alive and present, though we can hardly explain how. We together with them make up "the body of Christ" (a thought-provoking term, for it chooses the earthy term "body" over something more vaguely spiritual). This "body" is united, though it is composed of both visible and invisible members. It has real effects, in both the visible and invisible worlds.

Some Christians report encountering the presence of saints in ways similar to Metropolitan Anthony's encounter with Christ. Here's a story of a recent saint who had an encounter with the Virgin Mary that affected him in a way that seems paradoxical.

When St. Silouan (1866–1938) was a young man, he was sometimes devout, and other times drank and sang and brawled with companions in his Russian village. After a "period of wild living," according to his biographer, Abbot Sophrony Sakharov, he dozed off and had a revolting dream. He could feel a reptile crawling down his throat. He awoke to hear these words: "Just as you found it loathsome to swallow a snake in your dream, so I find your ways ugly to look upon."

Silouan "saw no one," Abbot Sophrony wrote. "He only heard the voice, extraordinarily sweet and beautiful; but for all its gentleness, the effect it had on him was revolutionary. He was convinced beyond doubt that he had heard the voice of the Mother of God herself, and to the end of his life he gave thanks to her for coming to lift him from his degradation.

"He would say, 'Now I see how sorry the Lord and His Mother are for people. Imagine—the Mother of God appearing from the skies to show a young man like me his sins!'"

It's striking that these words left Silouan with a lasting impression of sweetness. If anything, the message sounds firmly chastising, yet what Silouan felt was love. The words he received were immediately effective, and from that moment Silouan yearned to be a monk.

### Safety First

Any discussion of spiritual encounters must quickly be hedged with warning signs. I have a dramatic conversion story myself (much like Metropolitan Anthony's), and when I tell it I see that some audience members are moved, while others lean back and cross their arms skeptically over their chests. Oh, they believe that I *think* something happened, but that doesn't mean it did.

This skepticism is a healthy thing. In fact, it's a firm part of the Christian tradition. Visions, apparitions, and other mystical experiences must never be taken at face value; too many of them are products of emotional projection, while others are fabrications of the Evil One. Some have even humbler origins. Scrooge initially attributed Marley's ghost to indigestion, saying: "There is more of gravy about you than of the grave."

Taking false things for real is guaranteed to lead from bad to worse. Even legitimate experiences can tempt some people toward ballooning self-regard and progressive grand confusion.

When it comes to spiritual experiences, "safety first" means treating them with caution, and keeping handy a few grains of salt. It's good to have a spiritual father or mother, or at least a mature Christian friend, who can help with discernment. A common piece of advice is to simply ignore such occurrences, because with time the real thing has a way of establishing itself. If it's real, it will bear fruit by changing you for the better. You will find yourself becoming more patient and humble and loving toward other people. On the other hand, if its effect is to make you feel excited, it's probably a fraud.

And, for goodness' sake, don't go *seeking* such experiences. It's pretty much guaranteed that you'll experience something before long, and it will be the spiritual equivalent of getting an e-mail from a Nigerian widow who needs help with a transfer of money.

Seek the Lord, not his gifts, not his saints. Don't even seek a better prayer life. Seek him, and all things will be added unto you.

Because even when encounters are genuine, any beauty perceived is ultimately due to the presence of Christ. A saint is just an ordinary person who has been filled with the spirit of Christ. The quality that distinguishes one saint from another is like that of the light streaming from lanterns made of different shades of glass.

Each human being is an unrepeatable individual, and to fail to be a saint is to eternally deprive the kingdom of God of one irreplaceable shade of radiance. As the French philosopher Jean Bloy wrote, "There is but one sorrow: not to become a saint."

## Under her compassion

A thousand years ago there was a holy fool in Constantinople named Andrew. Like most "Fools for Christ," Andrew was in fact perfectly normal (even handsome and intelligent, his tradition holds). But he had taken on the challenging ascetic discipline of feigning madness, in order to acquire humility by allowing others to hold him in contempt. "We are fools for Christ's sake," wrote St. Paul (1 Cor. 4:10).

By choice, Andrew was homeless and utterly impoverished; he went about half-naked and ate only what people gave him. When he, in turn, gave to the poor, he would also mock them, as a strategy to avoid receiving thanks. Spending his days in humiliation and nights in constant prayer, Andrew honed his sense of the presence of God. He grew able to read into the souls of those around him, and would express these insights by symbolic actions or cryptic words that could penetrate the defenses of people too jaded to listen to a sermon. (We see the Hebrew prophets similarly using symbolic actions to convey their messages, sometimes at great cost to themselves. Isaiah went naked for three years, and Hosea remained faithful in a marriage to a prostitute.)

One freezing night Andrew had resorted to sleeping among the dogs on a dunghill, in an attempt to warm his body sufficiently to survive till morning. There an angel appeared to him, and carried him up to the "third heaven" that St. Paul saw (2 Cor. 12:2). It seemed to Andrew that the visit stretched to two weeks, as the angel showed him the courts of heaven. He even saw the Lord on his throne, "high and lifted up," just as the prophet Isaiah had described. Andrew said that the Lord spoke three words to him, and they filled him with unspeakable joy.

But Andrew did not see the Virgin Mary. At last he asked the angel to take him to her, but the angel replied, "Oh, she is not here! She goes down to the much-suffering earth, to help those in trouble and console those who sorrow."

Andrew's behavior made him well-known in the city, and a young man who saw through his stratagem, Epiphanius, became his companion and disciple. (We know Andrew's secret through Epiphanius, and also through Andrew's spiritual father. For someone engaged in a high-wire act like being a Fool-for-Christ, a spiritual mother or father is even more of a necessity.)

One evening Andrew and Epiphanius were attending an all-night prayer vigil at the church of the Virgin Mary, in a part of Constantinople called Blachernae. The city had gathered for fervent prayer, because a barbarian fleet was approaching the city and defeat seemed imminent.

The long hours passed, and hymns and chants filled the candle-lit darkness. Then, at four o'clock in the morning, Andrew turned to Epiphanius and asked in astonishment, "Do you see, brother, the Holy Theotokos, praying for the whole world?" Epiphanius answered, "I do, holy father, and am in awe."

As Andrew and Epiphanius watched, the Virgin Mary entered the church and proceeded to its center. She was accompanied by holy men and women from all centuries; Andrew and Epiphanius recognized St. John the Evangelist and St. John the Baptist among them. Mary knelt and prayed for a long time in tears. Then she stood and removed her veil and held it in her outstretched hands, rising and spreading it over the heads of the worshipers. The story of Andrew and Epiphanius says, "For a long time they observed the Protecting Veil spread over the people, and shining with flashes of glory."

The barbarians inexplicably retreated. The city was saved. And the feast of this event in AD 911 is observed every year on October 1.

Somewhere in Manchester a scrap of papyrus cataloged as number 470 is resting in a cool, dark, acid-free, and archivally optimum place. It's probable that no one handles it, and a cinch that no one reads it prayerfully. But for the man or woman who scribbled these words down, misspellings and all, so many centuries ago, it was one side of a continuing conversation. The response is what Andrew and Epiphanius saw, in the bleak hours before dawn in the church of Blachernae.

# Under Your Compassion

Under your
compassion
we take refuge,
Theotokos; do not
overlook our prayers
in the midst of tribulation,
but deliver us
from danger,
O only pure,
only blessed one.

# THREE

# Praising
# Mary's Honor

## *The extraordinary invention*

WE'LL NOW TURN TO A WORK WRITTEN A LITTLE LATER, around AD 520, a hymn that joyfully greets the Virgin and reflects on her conception of Jesus (this is why it's sung in Lent, close to the Feast of the Annunciation on March 25). This work is familiar to Eastern Orthodox Christians as the "Akathist Hymn" or the "Akathist Salutations to the Virgin." As before, I'm calling it by a title that identifies its contents, the "Annunciation Hymn."

About four centuries have passed since the time of the *Gospel of Mary*, and three since the "Compassion" prayer was inscribed on papyrus. First, we saw early Christians showing a tender, protective love for Mary; next, we witnessed their confidence that they can ask for her protection in turn.

With the Annunciation Hymn we see a new thing, and it is pretty dazzling. This long hymn captures dozens of

Scriptural allusions and theological paradoxes, all centering on the Virgin's pregnancy, and conveys them to the listener in a way that is concise, memorable, and brilliant as a jewel.

We noted the influence of oral transmission on the previous texts; this one is, on the contrary, a very carefully written work. But it is designed for an audience that will not be able to read it. Many of them are illiterate, and even those who can read aren't likely to acquire a written copy. The invention of the printing press is still 900 years away.

So the author-composer must make profound theological ideas accessible to an audience whose experience will be, literally, auditory. And, if they are to remember something of it, it can't be expressed in long, complex paragraphs. It needs to be condensed into nuggets—memorable nuggets that listeners can take home and think about later on. Setting it to music helps, of course, as we've all known since the time we learned our ABC's.

The Annunciation Hymn is regarded as the brightest example of a hymn form, the *kontakion*, which accomplishes these tasks magnificently. But St. Romanos, the developer of the kontakion and the author of this hymn, did not possess natural gifts that would equip him for this task. He was born in Syria about AD 475 and served as a deacon first in Beirut, then in Constantinople. There he was attached to the same church of the Virgin Mary in Blachernae where Andrew and Epiphanius would see the Theotokos 400 years later.

Tradition holds that young Romanos was very much out of his depth in the Eastern capital of the Roman Empire. The sophisticated clergy ridiculed his country manners, his lack of theological education, and particularly his sour singing voice. The elaborate liturgies required a great deal of vocal skill, and in Constantinople poor chanters were not welcome.

On the night before Christmas, Romanos prayed and wept in the church until sleep overcame him. In a dream the Theotokos appeared to him, and gave him a scroll that she instructed him to swallow. (In icons, this scroll is thoughtfully depicted in Romanos' native language, Arabic.) The next day, at the service for the Nativity of Christ, Romanos sang a new hymn in a voice of unearthly beauty:

Today the Virgin gives birth to the Inexpressible,
and the earth offers a cave to the Unapproachable;
angels and shepherds together give glory,
and the Magi are guided by a star,
when for our sakes was born, as a new babe,
The one who from eternity is God.

This hymn is still sung in Orthodox churches at the Christmas service every year. And the deacon who is now honored as St. Romanos the Melodist went on to write a thousand hymns, of which some 60 have been preserved.

Romanos developed the kontakion format by drawing on traditions from his homeland, particularly works by St. Ephrem the Syrian (AD 306–373). This kind of hymn is named for the spindle (*kontax*) around which a parchment scroll is wound, and as you may gather, *kontakia* can be very long, running from 18 to 30 verses or more.

The verses of a kontakion are called *houses*, that is *oikoi* (I don't know why). The first letter of each *oikos* forms an acrostic. In the hymn we'll read here it follows the letters of the Greek alphabet, but frequently it spells out the author's signature: "By the humble Romanos" or "A psalm by Romanos." (Listeners would scarcely be able to note these acrostics as the hymn flowed by; perhaps Romanos included them as an extra challenge to himself.) Each hymn is ruled by a rhythm that is established in the first oikos and persists throughout the work. During worship, chanters would present the body of the hymn, while the congregation would join in heartily on the refrain that comes at the end of each oikos.

Because kontakia are so very long, the common practice now is to sing only the first oikos. So if you visit an Eastern Orthodox church and notice "Kontakion of St. Michael the Archangel" (for example) in the bulletin, do not panic.

(Those of you who have read my book *First Fruits of Prayer: The Canon of St. Andrew* might be wondering where that other complex ancient hymn form, the canon, comes in. The answer is: about two hundred years later, around AD 720.)

As R. J. Schork points out in his marvelous book *Sacred Song from the Byzantine Pulpit: Romanos the Melodist*, a kontakion is a musical sermon: It "dramatically and emphatically recreates the 'plot' of the scriptural passage assigned to be read on the feast day. Then it explains any difficulties in the reading, applies this material to current theological controversies, and draws an appropriate Christian moral lesson."

Romanos' kontakia recount stories from the Bible or church history and have a notable dramatic flair. Listening to his kontakion on the temptation of Joseph (the Old Testament Joseph, the one with the "many-colored coat") must have been the sixth-century equivalent of going to the movies. As the wife of Joseph's master, Potiphar, wheedles her seduction, Joseph refutes her boldly. (Genesis 39:1 describes Potiphar as an "officer" of Pharaoh, but the Septuagint calls him Pharaoh's "eunuch"—which seems to give his wife a motive.) The contest between Joseph and Potiphar's wife ranges over 22 verses, and at the end of every stanza the congregation thunders: "For the eye that never sleeps sees everything!" (Think how your behavior might change if the jingle running through your head was this line sung by a few hundred friends, family members, and neighbors: "The eye that never sleeps sees everything!")

Romanos is also known for hymns in which characters engage in dialogue, such as *The Victory of the Cross*. This one calls to mind C. S. Lewis's *The Screwtape Letters*. It is the afternoon of the Crucifixion, and Hades is feeling sick, because something that feels like a wooden lance has pierced him. He tells the serpent-demon Belial that the cross up there means trouble, but Belial tells him not to be stupid. The cross, Belial sings, was his own idea, a clever instrument designed to defeat the Son of Mary. The two bicker and insult each other, but it gradually dawns on Belial that Hades is right. Catastrophe is at hand, and all their delicious captives will soon (here's the congregational refrain) "Return to Paradise!"

### The Annunciation Hymn

The kontakion we'll read here is Romanos' best known work. It is arranged as a series of greetings to Mary, and begins with the angel Gabriel's announcement of her pregnancy. The congregational refrain is a challenge to translate; it is modeled on Gabriel's words in Scripture, "Rejoice [Xaire], favored one [xarito'o]."

Romanos used "Xaire" in his refrain, but varied the term by which Mary is addressed; now it's "Xaire, nymphe anymphouete." You can get a general idea of this by noting that *nymph* means bride, and that it's followed by *anymph*. The prefix *a-* usually indicates an opposite, like *typical* and *atypical*, or *theist* and *atheist*.

But what's the opposite of "bride"? "Bride Unbride" has a Frankensteinian quality. The paradox the phrase wishes to convey is that, in the conception and birth of Jesus, Mary is genuinely a bride, and yet she remains a virgin. Other translators have offered "Unwedded Bride," "Bride without bridegroom," "Spouse Unespoused," and "Bride ever-virgin," without finding anything as evocative or neat. "Untouched Bride" says it, but is too clunky. I ended up choosing "Unmarried Bride" for its rhythm and repeating consonants, but I can't claim it's any more accurate.

This is just one example of how difficult it is to render this hymn in English. The kontakion has a linguistic brilliance no translation could adequately convey. Romanos has taken full advantage of Greek's capacity for paradox, and the poetry is pungently concise; garrulous, ungainly English can't really do it justice.

The hymn reminds me of the well-known fifteenth-century icon by St. Andrew Rublev, "The Holy Trinity," which depicts three angels seated around Abraham's table. The compressed radiance of that image, the lightness and interior brightness, resembles the effect of this hymn. I've polished my version to attempt some of Romanos' conciseness, and to honor (at least occasionally) his use of rhythm and subtly woven internal rhymes. There are now a million words in the English language, roughly ten times that of French, so English is capable of conveying just about any concept thoroughly and accurately. The biggest challenge in translation has been making it more concise.

This kontakion has a curious nickname, the "Akathist hymn." A *kathedra* is a chair, so this is the *a-kathist* or "not-sitting" hymn. About a century after this work was written, in AD 626, Constantinople was under siege, with enemy ships filling its surrounding harbor. The clergy marched around the city walls carrying an icon of the Theotokos, and a violent storm arose and destroyed the attacking navy. At that, the people flocked to the church of the Virgin and sang hymns all night long, without pausing to sit down and rest. This event established the custom of singing the hymn every year during Lent.

An *akathist* subsequently became an established form of hymn, a subset of kontakia; an akathist is distinguished by the pattern seen here, of a series of greetings or praises. Such akathist hymns have continued to be written over the centuries. A very beautiful "Akathist of Thanksgiving," a meditation on the beauty of Creation, was found on the body of a Russian Orthodox priest, Fr. Gregory Petrov, after his death in a Soviet prison camp in 1942. It had been circulating underground as a "samizdat" document, a Christian text forbidden by the Communist government. This hymn thanks God for such things as the brilliance of lightning viewed from the camp dining hall. The refrain is "Glory to God for all things," the last words of St. John Chrysostom as he died on the road to exile. Some Eastern Orthodox churches now use this beautiful, evocative akathist in their service for the eve of Thanksgiving.

When the Annunciation Hymn is offered as a worship service it is set in the context of regular evening prayers. Most of it is sung by the priest or by chanters, while everyone joins in on the "Alleluias" and "Rejoice, O Unmarried Bride!" While the hymn is appealing to read just as poetry, the experience of hearing it offered in song, in a church lit with candles and filled with incense, is when it fully comes alive. If you mark your calendar now, you won't forget to visit an Orthodox church next Lent and hear this hymn "in action."

### Focus on Pregnancy

The *Gospel of Mary* recounts a leisurely portion of Mary's life, but by the time of Romanos interest had focused more closely on her pregnancy. This was in response to a number of controversies in the fourth and fifth centuries over when, exactly, the Son of God began to be.

The priest Arius, around AD 320, taught that Christ existed before the universe, and in fact he created it and everything that exists—but he himself was created by God the Father. Christ had not existed always, from eternity: "There was a time when he was not," Arius said.

This notion roused great controversy, and in AD 325 the Emperor Constantine called together the clergy leaders of the whole world in the first Ecumenical Council. ("Ecumenical" here means the entire "household" of the inhabited world, the *oiko-menos*). They met in Nicea, a suburb of Constantinople, and after much debate produced a statement of faith, the Nicene Creed, which was signed by all but three of the 318 bishops attending. This creed states that Christ was not created by God; instead he is "begotten, not made" and "of one being with the Father."

Arianism continued to simmer for decades, and other arguments arose on similar questions. In the fifth century, the Patriarch of Constantinople, Nestorius, began to teach that there were two separate natures in Christ, human and divine. It was wrong to say "God suffered" or "God was crucified," as these events were experienced only by Christ's humanity. Likewise, the child in Mary's womb could not have been God, because "no one can bring forth a son older than herself," Nestorius said. So he opposed calling her "Theotokos," though that title had already been in use 200 years (as we saw previously, in the prayer "Under your compassion"). Instead, he recommended that she be called "Christotokos," indicating that she gave birth to Christ's human nature alone.

The third Ecumenical Council, meeting in Ephesus in AD 431, rejected Nestorius' argument. The Child in Mary's womb was both human and divine. The title "Theotokos" was then taken up victoriously, and is still the most common way to refer to Mary in the Eastern church.

*Theotokos* is often translated "Mother of God," but it more literally means "Birthgiver of God." We can recognize *Theos* as meaning *God*, while *tokos* comes from a verb meaning to carry in the womb and bear in childbirth.

While Mary is the only God-birthgiver, or Theotokos, we can all hope to become God-bearers, or Theophorus. The Greek verb used in this case shows up as *phor* or *pher* in English. St. Ignatius Theophorus was a "God-bearer," a martyr who was filled with God's light. St. Christopher, "Christ-bearer," carried the Christ child across a river.

It's not surprising that people in those centuries argued over the humanity and divinity of Jesus; the concept is a difficult one. Working out those difficulties and offering reliable definitions was a significant task for the defenders of orthodoxy. So it should be obvious that when they adopted the title *Theotokos*, they did not think it meant that Mary conceived the Trinity, or that she existed before God the Father, or any such bizarre notion. This title for Mary is primarily a statement about Jesus. It is designed to emphasize his divinity from the moment of conception.

Likewise, when we see an image of Mary as a young woman holding her baby, or as a pregnant woman with the child visible in her womb, we may think, "There's an icon of Mary." But that's not quite right; it's really an icon of the

Incarnation. Such images are not general portraits of her, but depictions of a turning point in the history of salvation.

### How can you know Scripture if you can't read?

Romanos wrote his hymn about a century after the Council of Chalcedon, and it communicates these complex theological truths in a concise and memorable way. But you might be thinking: isn't this awfully dense material to get across to a listening audience? Especially if many of them are uneducated and illiterate? How could Romanos expect them to understand it?

As we read his kontakia, we can see that Romanos' own knowledge of Scripture was extraordinary. In the infernal dialogue in "The Victory of the Cross," Hades and Belial recall an impressive range of biblical incidents in which wood was used for deliverance, from Jael's tent-peg to Haman's gallows to the stick Elisha threw in the Jordan to make a lost axe-head float. If I wanted to look up salvific incidents involving wood in the Hebrew Scriptures, I could open my Bible software and go zipping through in whichever translations and languages I chose. But as far as I know, Romanos didn't even own a concordance. It seems that he just really *knew* the Scriptures.

It seems that his audience did, too. Romanos would have aimed these hymns at their level of understanding. He took scriptural threads they'd heard often enough before, and pulled them together in a way that revealed exciting new patterns. How many Sunday worshipers today could keep up with such a cascade of references? Among the examples of salvation-by-wood, Romanos makes a passing allusion to Joshua's execution of five Amorite kings. Would you "get it," without looking it up? (I didn't.)

This familiarity with Scripture is even more impressive when you realize that most of the original audience—in fact, most Christians throughout history—didn't have a Bible at all, in the sense of owning a physical codex or scroll. Many of them could not even read. Yet they acquired familiarity with Scripture through the classic means employed from the time of Moses onward: by hearing it read aloud, by listening when it was chanted in worship. Throughout most of history, for most people, Scripture was not received by the eye but by the ear.

This seems an impossible method to us today. And it's true that earlier generations had some advantages over us when it came to absorbing information by ear. For one thing, they had much less to absorb. The place Scripture held in their memory was not flooded by extraneous passwords, PIN numbers, catch-phrases, and ad slogans. If a tune kept going through their head all day, it was likely to be one they'd heard in church.

Also, a pre-literate culture got more practice at memorizing, and discovered and used standard means of organizing material that made it easier to store and retrieve. For example, they made lists. It seems that some very early followers of Jesus made a list of his best-loved sayings, because it can (arguably) be discerned in the material shared by Matthew, Mark, and Luke. Scholars regret that no copy of this hypothetical document, which they call "Q," has been found. But maybe it never was a document. Maybe it was just passed along orally, from one living memory to the next.

(By the way, the existence of such "sayings lists" doesn't prove that Jesus was originally known only as a wise teacher, and his miracles were invented by later followers. We still enjoy collections of sayings. The existence of *The Wit & Wisdom of Winston Churchill* doesn't mean that his exploits in World War II were invented by adoring fans.)

The dependence on oral transmission of faith explains why public preaching was so important. St. Paul exhorts the Romans: "How are [people] to believe in [Christ] of whom they have never heard? And how are they to hear without a preacher? And how can they preach if they are not sent?" He concludes by citing the prophet Isaiah's words: "How beautiful are the feet of those who preach good news!"

You'll note there is nothing there about *reading* the Good News. The oral transmission of Christianity has a class-transcending side effect: an informed faith is not only for the educated. Any peasant could gain a good grasp of Christian teachings, just by attending worship. By listening to hymns like this one, by listening to the chanted Scripture readings and by studying the icons (a kind of picture Bible) covering a church's interior, any milkmaid could learn enough to tell the real Trinity from a shabby substitute.

And that common worship experience forged a common faith. Christians acknowledge Scripture as our highest authority, but that's shorthand for the *faith* that Scripture preserves. When the book is exploited apart from this faith, it malfunctions: a splinter group runs off a scary isolated verse, or a preacher ruminates endlessly on "Behold, my brother Esau is a hairy man." This Scriptural faith is not discovered by pitting one bright interpreter against another; that just provokes argument. Instead it is found, fresh and living, in the collective memory of the worshiping body of Christ.

When worship doesn't change, the faith doesn't change. Even today, someone who wants to find out what Eastern Christians believe about, say, the Ascension of Christ is not sent to a catechism or a tome of systematic theology. Instead, they're invited to look at how Eastern Christians approach this topic when they worship. What hymns do they sing when this feast rolls around? What clues can be picked up from the icon that depicts the Ascension?

To worshipers, the beliefs they honor in such forms feel organically their own. These points of faith haven't been imposed by a bossy outsider, and they aren't subject to unexpected "updatings" that immediately feel dated. Instead, these beliefs come up from the believers' own roots, and as a result they will defend them with their lives. It's estimated that more Christians were martyred under Communism than in the whole preceding history of the faith.

When the church was still young, an attentive, informed laity was able to resist strange moral and theological ideas, even when these were propounded by clergy. St. Basil the Great describes fourth-century worshipers who met "in the open air, in heavy rain, in the snow, . . . and under the blazing heat of the sun" rather than enter churches held by priests who were followers of Arius.

*Extravagance*

The Annunciation Hymn focuses on a particular area of Christian theology that had been thoroughly tested in prior centuries, the full humanity and divinity of Jesus Christ, and the subtle paradoxes of the Incarnation. The more Christians thought about it, the more wonder they felt at the bare fact of Mary's pregnancy. The God who made the entire universe, who holds Creation in the palm of his hand, was somehow voluntarily enclosed in the space of her womb. ("He made your body more spacious than the heavens!" another hymn would rejoice.)

Everything earthly about Christ's body—everything that's *us*—was supplied by and through Mary's own body. For this role, Mary is cheered like a hometown hero who made good. As the first step in our rescue, God invited the participation of a real human being, one who had an ordinary human body, which ate and itched and grew tired just like ours. His plan required the partnership of a regular person, and he didn't choose someone who was powerful, strong or famous; he chose a girl. Everything turned on that moment, and Mary said yes. That seems enough to warrant a ticker-tape parade.

Whereas the *Gospel of Mary* was plainspoken and homey, this hymn is glorious, and the terms used to praise Mary are elaborate. She is now hailed as "mother of the unsetting star," "dawn of the mystic day," "pillar of virgins," "gate of salvation," and much more.

Some readers may feel uncomfortable with this. It helps to recognize that this praise of Mary is not *replacing* similar terms of praise to God. It is kind of like "counting your blessings." If you prayerfully detail all the wonderful things God has done for you, you aren't setting them up as a rival to God. If anything, they increase your love of God, who has done great things.

What's more, this language is strongly typological, as we saw in the *Gospel of Mary*. There, Mary was seen foreshadowed by the Ark and the Holy of Holies. That imagery continues here, and is joined by many more Scriptural allusions. Mary's virgin conception, in particular, has been considered in light of the Hebrew Scriptures. In this miracle, God altered the course of nature by his own will and power. Yet he did this while preserving the delicate harmony of the female human body, his own creation. This great miracle waited on the permission of a girl, and was achieved without compromising the integrity of her vulnerable natural body.

The early Christians found the Hebrew Scriptures to be overflowing with references to this coming miracle:

The ladder that Jacob saw, which reached from heaven to earth (Gen. 28:12)

The bush that Moses saw, which was burning but not consumed (Ex. 3:2)

The golden urn of manna that Moses preserved, so that future generations could see the bread God provided in the wilderness (Ex. 16:32)

The rock that Moses struck, which then produced a fountain of water (Ex. 17:6)

The rod of Aaron, which blossomed though it was dry (Num. 17:8)

The stone that Daniel saw, which was cut from a mountain by no human hand (Dan. 2:34)

The east gate that Ezekiel saw, through which the Lord entered and which would henceforth be shut (Ezek. 43:4, 44:2)

Overall, praise of Mary is becoming more lavish. We misunderstand if we hear these honors put forth as precise theological assertions. The Western Christian way of thinking about theology was powerfully shaped by the work of St. Thomas Aquinas, who in the thirteenth century developed an approach that treats faith like a science. However, this hymn precedes him by 700 years, and comes from a very different culture.

Here the goal is not so much understanding God in a rational way as directly experiencing him. This worship starts with the assumption that God is present throughout Creation, sustaining our every heartbeat, hearing our every thought, perceptible in the beauty and love we encounter in the material world. And it's assumed that trying to *think* about this makes you trip over your own feet. As St. Maximos the Confessor (580–662) put it, "direct experience of a thing suspends rational knowledge of it, and direct perception of a thing renders the conceptual knowledge of it useless."

So worshipers expected to offer this hymn, not just dutifully about Mary, but joyously *to* her, while participating in some inexpressible communication with her. They would do this while standing in the presence of God, in the midst of a company of family and friends, saints and angels, seen and unseen. This encounter would take place whether or not they felt moved emotionally. (We tend to get "experience" and "emotion" mixed when we talk about faith, but they're different things. Having emotions about going to the dentist is not the same thing as actually *going* to the dentist.) The experience is primary, and any emotions or thoughts that arise are unimportant. What's important is to participate— to be fully there.

So the context of these praises is a celebration, and they are a suitably glorious outpouring for that purpose, much like the language a lover bestows on his beloved. If you were to hear one of these Christians singing to Mary, "You alone are our only hope," you would probably ask him, "Do you really believe that Mary is your *only* hope?" He might well reply, "Of course not, where did you get that idea?" People in love say extravagant things.

## Only human—but that was enough

Mary was ardently loved by these early Christians, and respected for her holiness, but they didn't get her mixed up with God. If Jesus himself "in every respect has been tempted as we are, yet without sin" (Heb. 4:15), she cannot have done better than that. St. Ambrose (d. AD 397)believed that Mary successfully resisted sin, but that she was "not a stranger to sinful temptations. God alone is without sin."

The whole point of her role in God's plan is that she represented us; she was an authentic human being. And though the early Christians saw in her an exemplary model of holiness, they didn't think she had magical powers, or that she knew everything in the mind of God.

A poignant story about her gradually unfolding comprehension of God's plan can be discerned in the Gospels. When this teenage girl had had a few days to absorb the angel's words, she responded to her cousin Elizabeth's greeting by singing a hymn, "My soul magnifies the Lord." In it, she quoted boldly from Scriptures she'd been hearing all her life. Skipping through the psalms and prophets, she proclaimed that the Lord was about to cast down the mighty, raise up the poor, and feed the hungry; that he has helped his servant Israel, remembered his mercy, and kept his promise to Abraham's descendants.

Like all of Israel, Mary was looking for the Messiah who would put things right, ending the Roman occupation and restoring justice. At last, the Messiah is conceived!

So it's no wonder that Mary and Joseph "marveled" when Simeon spoke to them in the temple, because he said some surprising things. As Simeon held the baby Jesus in his arms, he spoke of him as a light to the Gentiles, and not just the glory of Israel. Instead of predicting military victory, Simeon said that the child would be spoken against, and that "thoughts out of many hearts" would be revealed. What would that have to do with defeating Roman oppressors? This would not make sense until Jesus began to teach that outward behavior is worthless without a healed heart. And it was yet more unsettling when Simeon said to Mary, "a sword will pierce through your soul also."

As time passed, it no doubt became clear to her that the things she'd been taught the Messiah would do were not what was going to happen. The predictions she made in her joyous song did not come true in anything like the way she'd expected. A few decades after Christ's earthly life ended, the Roman army laid siege to Jerusalem. At the end, the Jewish poor had not been filled with good things; they had been emptied to the point of starvation, and there were even rumors of cannibalism. The lowly poor were not lifted up; they were slaughtered, often by competing Jewish gangs. The mighty Roman Emperor was not cast down from his throne. Instead he enjoyed a victory parade in Rome, where the entertainment included the execution of Jewish rebel leaders.

One indicator that Mary's song is authentic, that it really is what she said at the time, is that it so poignantly does *not* predict what lay ahead in Israel's political history. Only later did Jesus' followers comprehend that his kingship is truly "not of this world." His warfare is truly "not against flesh and blood." If Jesus had seized earthly power, even for a just cause, its effects would have been as temporary and morally ambivalent as any other use of power. If Mary's song of praise prophesied material bounty for the oppressed of her land, it is a prophecy that didn't come true.

But, like others throughout Scripture, Mary had spoken a truth that meant something more than she understood. Jesus had a greater Enemy in mind, the Mighty One who had enslaved humanity in Death from the beginning. His claws were in the brains of Israel's Roman oppressors, and behind every act of malice since time began. That one was cast down from his throne, and this conferred on all humanity a victory more profound and penetrating and universal than any merely political power could achieve.

In the course of Jesus' busy ministry, the glimpses of Mary are few and brief. In the third chapter of Mark, we see her accompanying (perhaps reluctantly) a group of Jesus' brothers who have heard a rumor that he is insane, and have come to cart him away.

Who can comprehend what must have been in her heart in those days, or how severely her faith was tried? Surely she always loved and obeyed God, and always loved her son. But she would have had reason enough to feel confused and dismayed. Perhaps she wondered if she had misunderstood God all along, or if he was not really the kind of God she thought she knew.

Romanos' kontakion "The Lament of the Theotokos," sung on Friday in Holy Week, depicts Mary following as Christ carries his cross. She is bewildered by sorrow, and asks:

> "Where are you going, my Child?
> Why do you run so swiftly?
> Is there another wedding in Cana,
> and are you hastening there to turn the water into wine?"

He is indeed going to a wedding feast, and he will provide the wine. Mary continues:

> "Shall I go with you, my Child, or shall I wait for you?
> Speak some word to me, O Word;
> do not pass me by in silence."

At the brutal cross her grief turns wild:

> With a mother's love she wept
> and bitterly her heart was wounded.
> She groaned in anguish from the depth of her soul,
> and in her grief she struck her face and tore her hair.
> And beating her breast she cried,
> "Woe is me, my divine Child!
> Woe is me, Light of the World!
> Why do you vanish from my sight,
> O Lamb of God?"

Then the hosts of angels were seized with trembling,
and they said, "O Lord beyond our understanding,
glory to you."

It is this same woman, so holy and God-loving, so real and
human, who is lauded with extravagant praise. She is held up
as the example for all Christians to imitate. She is honored for
one particular moment in her holy life: she said yes to God.

# The Annunciation Hymn

*The Annunciation Hymn*

1 As Luke tells us, "The angel Gabriel was sent from God . . .
to a virgin betrothed to a man whose name was Joseph"
(Lk. 1:26–27).

2 The angels are sometimes called "bodiless powers," emphasizing
that these creatures who serve God's will do not participate in
the matter of the universe. The astonishment of the angels at
Christ's Incarnation is a common theme in Eastern hymns. As
Gabriel cries out to Mary with a "bodiless voice," he perceives
the "bodily form" of the immaterial and immortal Son of God
beginning to appear.

3 Gabriel's first address to the Virgin considers the conception of
Christ in light of the earliest moments of human history, and
recollects the Creation and Adam and Eve's fall, as found in
Genesis 1–3.

4 "Creation is reborn." In "On the Incarnation" (AD 320), St.
Athanasius says that when a portrait is damaged it is not
thrown away, "but the subject of the portrait must go in and
sit for it again, and then the likeness is redrawn on the same
material." Christ's Incarnation likewise redraws the "image of
God" on material human life. He fills damaged human nature
with divinity, healing and restoring it to its first beauty.

## Oikos 1

An Archangel was sent from heaven to cry "Rejoice!" to the
Theotokos;[1]
and, O Lord, as he saw you taking bodily form
at the sound of his bodiless voice,
he stood wonder-struck[2]
crying out such things as these:

Rejoice, for through you joy will shine forth,
Rejoice, for through you bondage will cease,
Rejoice, arising of fallen Adam,
Rejoice, release of weeping Eve,[3]
Rejoice, height surpassing all human thought,
Rejoice, depth profoundly beyond angels' sight,
Rejoice, for you furnish a kingly throne,
Rejoice, for you hold him who upholds all,
Rejoice, star in which the sun is revealed,
Rejoice, womb in which God takes on flesh,
Rejoice, for through you creation is reborn,
Rejoice, for through you we worship the Creator![4]
Rejoice, O Unmarried Bride!

5 Luke writes, "But she was greatly troubled at the saying, and considered in her mind what sort of greeting this might be" (Luke 1:29). The Gospel of Luke presents the events of Christ's conception and birth from Mary's point of view. Luke was an educated man, a physician and friend of St. Paul (Col. 4:14), born in Antioch and probably fluent in both Greek and Aramaic. The Gospel he wrote is the most literary of the four. Luke is something of an investigative reporter; he explains in his first chapter that his aim was to "compile a narrative of the things . . . delivered to us by those who from the beginning were eyewitnesses" (Lk. 1:1–2).

One of the most important eyewitnesses "from the beginning" would, of course, be the Virgin Mary. Tradition holds that Luke paid her a visit, while she was peacefully living out her last days in the home of St. John. She is the only possible source for the events of the Annunciation, or for details like "Mary kept all these things, pondering them in her heart" (Lk. 2:19). It is appealing to imagine the elderly peasant woman and the bright young man sitting together, he taking rapid notes while she draws up from the well of memory the unforgettable moments of decades before.

6 The Gospel of St. John identifies the miracle at the wedding in Cana, in which Christ turned water to wine, as "the first of his signs" (Jn. 2:11), but the angel here points to the Incarnation as a miracle preceding even that.

7 Jacob "dreamed that there was a ladder set up on the earth, and the top of it reached to heaven" (Gen. 28:12). This ladder foreshadows the Virgin's role in enabling God to descend in human form. Jesus said to the Apostle Nathaniel, "Truly, truly I say to you, you will see heaven opened, and the angels of God ascending and descending upon the Son of Man" (Jn. 1:51).

8 Gabriel's emphasis on silence and stillness is fitting for a miracle that cannot be expressed in words.

## OIKOS 2

Seeing herself pure, the holy maiden
spoke to Gabriel boldly:
The strange wonder you tell appears hard to my soul,
for you speak of a birth
from a seedless conception, crying aloud:
Alleluia![5]

## OIKOS 3

Seeking to know what cannot be known,
the Virgin spoke to the one who came to her:
Tell me, how can a chaste womb bear a son?
But in fear he replied,
crying out only this:

Rejoice, initiate of ineffable counsel,
Rejoice, faith keeping silence in stillness,
Rejoice, inauguration of Christ's mighty deeds,[6]
Rejoice, crown of his excellent teachings,
Rejoice, ladder of heaven by which God descends,[7]
Rejoice, bridge that guides the earthly to heaven,
Rejoice, jubilant wonder to angels,
Rejoice, disastrous wound to the demons,
Rejoice, for you give birth to Light inexpressible,
Rejoice, for you told no one how it was done,[8]
Rejoice, understanding surpassing the wise,
Rejoice, dawn enlightening faithful minds,
Rejoice, O Unmarried Bride!

9 The angel told Mary, "The power of the Most High will overshadow you" (Lk. 1.35). Readers of the Septuagint found a
foreshadowing in Habakkuk 3:3, "God shall come out of . . .
a mountain overshadowed."

10 Luke writes, "And when Elizabeth heard the greeting of Mary,
the babe leaped in her womb" (Lk. 1:41). Romanos here imag-
ines what the joyous leaping of the unborn John would be
communicating if expressed in words.

11 God instructed Moses to make a "mercy seat," a golden
platform, and place it on top of the ark (the golden chest
containing the tablets of the Law). On the mercy seat were set
two carved cherubim (plural of *cherub*), facing each other
with wings touching. This was understood to be the throne of
the invisible God, the place where humans find mercy and are
reconciled to God. Mary herself now becomes the mercy seat
of the whole world. In icons that depict the Ark being carried
into Solomon's temple, an image of the Theotokos is shown
engraved on the side of the Ark.

12 "Assurance" is an attempt to translate *parresia*, which means
being able to speak freely—for example, a commoner who has
been so welcomed by a king that he feels he can say honestly
whatever is on his mind. This is one of the first steps in prayer.

## OIKOS 4

Then power from the Most High
overshadowed[9] the maiden unto conception;
and her fruitful womb was revealed as a fertile field
to all who wish to reap salvation,
as they sing:
Alleluia!

## OIKOS 5

Enclosing God within her womb,
the virgin hastened to Elizabeth,
whose unborn babe at once recognized her greeting,
and rejoiced with leaping as if with songs,[10]
crying out to the Theotokos:

Rejoice, branch of unwithering bud,
Rejoice, orchard of unfading fruit,
Rejoice, sustainer of him who sustains human love,
Rejoice, care-giver of him who cares for our life,
Rejoice, farmland rich with boundless compassion,
Rejoice, table laden with bountiful mercies,
Rejoice, for you awaken the meadows of joy,
Rejoice, for you offer a harbor for souls,
Rejoice, worthy incense of intercession,
Rejoice, mercy seat of all the world,[11]
Rejoice, good pleasure of God toward mortals,
Rejoice, assurance[12] of mortals toward God,
Rejoice, O Unmarried Bride!

13 The first letter of St. Peter says Jesus is like "a lamb without blemish or spot" (1 Pet. 1:19). God's instructions for the Israelites at the first Passover required a lamb "without blemish" (Ex. 12:5).

14 Jesus said, "I am the good shepherd" (Jn. 10:11).

15 The shepherds, naturally, draw their analogies from sheep-folds and lambs. The phrase here is literally "logical sheep," but the term is misleading; it does not imply "rational" so much as "enlightened." The "sheep" who receive the light of Christ have been freed from delusion and darkness of mind, and can newly perceive God permeating and ordering his good Creation.

16 Psalm 96:11 says, "Let the heavens be glad, and let the earth rejoice."

17 "Death and Hades gave up the dead in them" (Rev. 20:13).

## OIKOS 6

A storm of doubtful thoughts roiled within the prudent Joseph,
for he looked on you unwedded
and he feared a stolen union, O Blameless One;
but on learning your child-bearing
was of the Holy Spirit, he said:
Alleluia!

## OIKOS 7

Hearing angels singing of Christ's coming in the flesh,
the shepherds ran as to a shepherd;
and when they saw the spotless lamb[13]
who had pastured in the womb of Mary,
they sang her praise and said:

Rejoice, mother of both Lamb and Shepherd,[14]
Rejoice, fold of sheep made wise,[15]
Rejoice, sure wall against foes unseen,
Rejoice, opener of Paradise-gates,
Rejoice, for the heavens exult with the earth,[16]
Rejoice, for the earthly sing praise with the heavens,
Rejoice, never-silenced voice of apostles,
Rejoice, never-conquered courage of martyrs,
Rejoice, firm foundation of faith,
Rejoice, bright revelation of grace,
Rejoice, through you Hades is stripped bare,[17]
Rejoice, through you we are gloriously robed,
Rejoice, O Unmarried Bride!

18 St. Paul writes to Timothy that God "dwells in unapproachable light" (1 Tim. 6:16).

19 Job says, "Thy hands fashioned and made me" (Job 10:8).

20 St. Paul writes to the Philippians: "he . . . emptied himself, taking the form of a servant" (Phil. 2:6–7).

21 The "sons of the Chaldees" are seen as Zoroastrians, fire-worshipers, and their address to Mary is full of references to sunlight and fire.

22 Mary extinguishes the fire of evil, and brings light to true worshipers. The parallelism in these two lines is not as obvious as it would have been to someone who lived before the invention of the electric bulb. For most of history, light inevitably meant fire; any reference to God as light would carry a note of respect for fire's uncompromising power. The idea of light that is cool, harmless, and tame would be as strange to this hymn's earlier hearers as the idea of "dry water" is to us.

23 Literally, "muddy" or "slimy" works. The Greek term is *borboros*, a fine echo of *barbaros* in the preceding line.

24 I have used the word *cravings* to translate the Greek word *pathon* here. It is usually translated "passions" in spiritual literature, but the literal meaning is "sufferings." It refers to the habitual cravings that make us suffer, impulses like anger and greed, which unsettle us, disrupt our peace in God, and damage our relationships. The term embraces both the imperious power of the urges, and the passive helplessness we feel under such attacks. The singular is *pathos*.

## OIKOS 8

The Magi beheld a star leading toward God
and they followed its brilliance,
and holding it as a lamp they went seeking a king.
And having approached the Unapproachable,[18]
with rejoicing they cried to him:
Alleluia!

## OIKOS 9

The sons of the Chaldees beheld in the hands of the Virgin
the one whose hand fashioned all of mankind.[19]
And knowing him as master, though in the form of a servant,[20]
they hastened with gifts to honor him,
and to the Blessed they cried:

Rejoice, mother of the unsetting star,[21]
Rejoice, dawn of the mystic day,
Rejoice, for you extinguish the flames of deceit,
Rejoice, for you enlighten the Trinity's worshipers,[22]
Rejoice, downfall of the tyrant who hates mankind,
Rejoice, arising of Christ, the Lord who loves mankind,
Rejoice, liberation from barbarous rituals,
Rejoice, deliverance from ugly works,[23]
Rejoice, the end of the worship of fire,
Rejoice, deliverance from fiery cravings,[24]
Rejoice, guide of the faithful to chastity,
Rejoice, delight of all generations,
Rejoice, O Unmarried Bride!

25 A *lerode*, one who says silly, nonsensical things. When the women returned from Christ's empty tomb and told the apostles what they had seen, the apostles dismissed their words as *leros* (Lk. 24:11).

26 When the fugitive family arrives in Egypt, the presence of the infant Christ causes idols to topple. This recalls Isaiah's prophecy: "Behold, the LORD is riding on a swift cloud and comes to Egypt; and the idols of Egypt will tremble at his presence" (Isa. 19:1). The coming of this Jewish family to Egypt frees the Egyptians who had been enslaved to idols, just as the Jews were freed from slavery in Egypt, thousands of years before. Christianity was established in Egypt very early; the Coptic Church traces its founding to the preaching of St. Mark in Alexandria, in AD 45.

27 Idol worship is not merely forbidden; it is a fraud. The idea that a physical object has magical powers twists the inborn human faculty for worship into something ruled by manipulation and fear. It is hard for us to conceive of how liberating it was for ancient peoples to discover that the real God transcended all those dumb, terrifying objects—and, what's more, that he loved them, and had personally come to earth, and died to free them from death. There's a reason that the Gospel was called the "Good News."

28 "The noetic Pharaoh" is the Evil One, who meddles in the realm of spiritual perception (the arena of the *nous*, hence the adjective *noetic*) to capture human minds. By misleading, confusing, intimidating, and disturbing human beings, he wrecks their ability to perceive the world in God-centered tranquility.

From here through the rest of this oikos, the analogies are all to the experience of the Jews when freed from Egypt: they escaped Pharaoh, were given water from a rock, were led by a fiery pillar at night and a cloud by day, ate manna, and came into a promised land flowing with milk and honey.

29 In our rainy climates, a cloud suggests disappointment: "a cloud came over the gathering." But in arid lands where the

## Oikos 10

God-bearing heralds the Magi became when they
came back to Babylon; they fulfilled the prophecy,
and proclaimed you to all as the Christ.
And Herod they abandoned as a babbler[25]
who knew not how to sing:
Alleluia!

## Oikos 11

Lighting in Egypt the lamp of truth,
you cast out the darkness of falsehood, O Savior.
For those idols could not resist your might and they fell;
and those who were freed from them[26]
cried aloud to the Theotokos:

Rejoice, uplifter of mankind,
Rejoice, downfall of demons,
Rejoice, trampler of misleading error,
Rejoice, exposer of fraudulent idols,[27]
Rejoice, sea that drowns the noetic Pharaoh,[28]
Rejoice, rock that refreshes those thirsting for life,
Rejoice, fiery pillar, leading those in darkness,
Rejoice, shelter of the world, broader than a cloud,[29]
Rejoice, nourishment better than manna,
Rejoice, minister of holy delight,
Rejoice, good land that had been promised,
Rejoice, from which flows honey and milk,
Rejoice, O Unmarried Bride!

sun beats down mercilessly, a cloud is a sign of blessing, and an emblem of shelter and safety.

30 Simeon was a citizen of Jerusalem, aged and devout, who had received a promise from God that he would not die before seeing the "anointed one," the Christ. He was in the temple when Mary and Joseph brought in the infant Jesus, to make the customary presentation of a first-born son with the sacrifice of two doves.

31 Mary's virginity before and after childbirth are here understood as the inbreaking of a new kind of Creation. Another hymn to Mary says, "Wherever God wills, the order of nature is overthrown."

32 Chastity is here paired with immortality; a body that is untouched and virginal is like one that has escaped the corruption of death.

33 Monastic life, by definition chaste, aims to replicate the life of angels.

34 The term again is *parresia*. We can imagine a person who is too intimidated to speak in the presence of a king, who feels naked of worth. But the part Mary played in salvation is a reminder of God's loving outreach toward humanity, and provides a robe of confidence.

35 Readers of C. S. Lewis's *The Four Loves* would recognize the word translated "tenderness" as *storge*, the kind of love that characterizes family life. Mary's motherly tenderness strengthens our resistance to tormenting desires.

## OIKOS 12

Very near to departing from this deceitful age
was Simeon when you were brought to him as a babe,[30]
but he recognized you as perfect God.
Overwhelmed, therefore, by your ineffable wisdom,
he cried out:
Alleluia!

## OIKOS 13

A new Creation was revealed by the Creator
to us whom he had made;
for he budded from a seedless womb
and preserved it as it was, unchanged,[31]
so that we who see this wonder may cry aloud and sing:

Rejoice, flower of incorruption,
Rejoice, crown of chastity,[32]
Rejoice, for you prefigure the bright Resurrection,
Rejoice, for you model the life of the angels,[33]
Rejoice, fruitful tree, feeding the faithful,
Rejoice, leafy tree, sheltering many,
Rejoice, for you bore a guide for the wayward,
Rejoice, for you delivered a deliverer of captives,
Rejoice, supplicant before the just Judge,
Rejoice, mercy for many who stumble,
Rejoice, robe adorning those stripped of assurance,[34]
Rejoice, tenderness conquering unwanted desires,[35]
Rejoice, O Unmarried Bride!

36 Romanos is at pains to communicate that Christ's life on earth did not mean he was absent from heaven; it was a "condescension" rather than a mere "descent." This is a difficult concept, but when it is expressed in song and in a memorable turn of phrase, any worshiper could take hold of it and retain it for further contemplation.

37 A brilliant paradox, more tidy in Greek: Mary is the *chora* of God, who is himself *achora*.

38 Because of the two carved golden cherubim atop the "mercy seat," God is often hailed in Scripture as "enthroned above the cherubim" (2 Kings 19:15; 1 Chronicles 13:6; Isaiah 37:16). Seraphim (singular, *seraph*) on the other hand are mentioned only once in Scripture: Isaiah recounts a vision he had in the temple, in which he saw God on a high throne, surrounded by six-winged angels who sang "Holy, Holy, Holy" (Isa. 6:1–7).

## Oikos 14

Having seen this strange birth-giving,
let us become strangers to the world
and be brought over into heaven.
The Most High appeared on earth in humble human form,
for he wished to draw on high those who cry out unto him:
Alleluia!

## Oikos 15

Wholly present among those below,
yet in no way absent from those above,
was the Word that cannot be encircled by words;
for thus did God condescend, and not merely descend to a
different place.[36]
He was born from a God-receiving virgin, who hears these
words:

Rejoice, homeland of the boundless God,[37]
Rejoice, doorway of sacred mystery,
Rejoice, dubious myth to the faithless,
Rejoice, confident boast of the faithful,
Rejoice, all-holy chariot of him above the cherubim,
Rejoice, all-virtuous home of him above the seraphim,[38]
Rejoice, for you draw opposites into harmony,
Rejoice, for you join childbirth with virginity,
Rejoice, you through whom transgression is annulled,
Rejoice, you through whom Paradise is opened,
Rejoice, key of the kingdom of Christ,

39 The term *angel* means simply "messenger." The traditional Christian understanding (adopted from the fifth-century writings of St. Dionysius) is that there are nine ranks of these heavenly beings, of which angels and archangels are in the lowest order, while cherubim and seraphim are in the highest.

40 The *philo-sophers* (lovers of wisdom) are *a-sophos* and the *techno-logists* (crafters of logic) are *a-logos*. The early Christians did not admire the Greek philosophers as much as Christians did later on in the West. In the early centuries, the term *philosopher* meant a pagan opponent of Christianity, and a clever debater at that. Saints' victories over "philosophers" are still celebrated in some of the Eastern Church's hymns. For example, the kontakion of St. Sophia says, "Sophia, the name-sake of wisdom, by grace has shown all that Greek wisdom is foolishness." And the kontakion of St. Catherine, who bested philosophers in debate, tells us that she "trampled the serpent down and spat on the knowledge of the eloquent."

41 This is a wonderful series of lines, which turns from the cleverly woven (*ploke*) rhetorical traps of Athenian philosophers to the humble nets of the apostolic fishermen. You can almost feel the journey: into the net, up from the depths, into the light, onto the ship, safe in the harbor. The startling image of orators "voiceless as fish" now gets tied into an evolving metaphor.

Rejoice, hope of eternal good things,
Rejoice, O Unmarried Bride!

## OIKOS 16

Every order of angels[39] was amazed at your mighty work
when you assumed human nature;
for they saw the one who is unapproachable as God
become approachable to all as man,
dwelling among us, and hearing from all:
Alleluia!

## OIKOS 17

We see eloquent orators voiceless as fish
before you, Theotokos, for they cannot explain
how you are a virgin and yet can give birth;
but in awe at the mystery,
in faith we cry out:

Rejoice, vessel of God's wisdom,
Rejoice, treasury of his providence,
Rejoice, for you show the worldly-wise barren of wisdom,
Rejoice, for you prove the logicians empty of logic,[40]
Rejoice, subtle debaters are turned into fools,
Rejoice, myth-makers must wither away,
Rejoice, for you smash the traps of Athenians,
Rejoice, for you fill the nets of the fishermen,[41]
Rejoice, drawing us up from the depths of ignorance,

42 God became like us in order to reach us. Once I saw a hawk
fly into a window and drop the young squirrel it was carrying.
As I walked further on, I began to hear the squirrel's parent
squeaking and searching for it. I couldn't figure out any way to
bring them closer together; for them to trust me, I would have
had to become a squirrel. God had to become one of us. He
calls "from like to like," and in return hears our Alleluia.

Rejoice, bringing many to bright understanding,
Rejoice, ship of those who yearn for salvation,
Rejoice, harbor for those faring over life's sea,
Rejoice, O Unmarried Bride!


## OIKOS 18

Desiring to save the world, the world-maker
came down upon it by his own free will.
As God he is our shepherd from eternity,
yet for our sake he showed himself in our own likeness;
and having called from like to like,[42] as God he hears:
Alleluia!


## OIKOS 19

You are a battlement to virgins
and to all who run to you, Virgin Theotokos;
for the maker of heaven and earth
prepared you, O Pure One, dwelling in your womb
and teaching all to call to you:

Rejoice, pillar of virgins,
Rejoice, gate of salvation,
Rejoice, beginning of noetic restoration,
Rejoice, bestowal of God's benevolence,
Rejoice, new birth for those conceived in shame,
Rejoice, new understanding for those whose minds were
plundered,

43 Sins are the end result of a process that begins long before, with damaged or corrupted thoughts and perceptions. Temptations are the Evil One's attempts to sow this disordered thinking, a project calculated to hit each person in his weak point. "Each person is tempted when he is lured and enticed by his own desire. Then desire when it has conceived gives birth to sin; and sin when it is full-grown brings forth death" (Jms. 1:14–15).

44 These lines make it clear that the Virgin is not herself the focus of salvation, but a beloved and admirable friend who helps us to that goal: she is bridal chamber, nursing-mother, and betrother.

Rejoice, for you destroy the seducer of thoughts,[43]
Rejoice, for you give birth to the Sower of chastity,
Rejoice, bridal chamber of a virgin marriage,
Rejoice, for you wed believers to the Lord,
Rejoice, fair nursing-mother of virgins,
Rejoice, betrother of holy souls,[44]
Rejoice, O Unmarried Bride!

## Oikos 20

Every hymn that seeks to recount the multitudes
of your many mercies must fail; for even if we offered songs
as numerous as the sands, O Holy King,
we accomplish nothing worthy of what you have given us,
who cry to you:
Alleluia!

## Oikos 21

We behold the holy Virgin as a light-bearing beacon
shining on those in darkness;
for by kindling the immaterial light she guides all to divine
knowledge,
illuminating the mind with radiance,
and her we honor with this cry:

Rejoice, ray of the noetic sun,
Rejoice, beam of the unsetting moon,
Rejoice, lightning flashing upon our souls,

45 The "enemies" are the lying demons, in hymnography as in
Christian reading of the Psalms. A line like "Happy shall he be
who takes your little ones and dashes them against the rock!"
(Ps. 137:9) may have had a horrifying meaning when it was
penned, but to Christians it now means vigilance against the
Evil One and the sneaky little devil-planted thoughts and
deeds that infiltrate and poison our relationship with God.
An Eastern Christian hymn in honor of the Holy Cross
expresses a similar idea: "Through the Cross we have been
found worthy to smash the heads of invisible enemies."

46 The laver was a very large bronze vessel, in which priests
washed their hands and feet before participating in sacrifices.
To Christians it became an emblem of the baptismal font,
and St. Paul uses the same term in his letter to Titus: "the
laver of regeneration and renewal in the Holy Spirit"
(author's translation, Titus 3:5).

47 A wine-bowl, or *krater*, was a large bowl in which wine and
water were mixed before serving. "Wisdom has . . . mixed her
wine, she has also set her table" (Prov. 9:1–2). This oikos
begins with images of light, then moves to images of water, and
proceeds from the baptismal font to joyous feasting.

48 In this beautiful summary God does it all: the "Creditor"
comes to those who had fled from him and cancels their debt.

Rejoice, thunder smashing our enemies,[45]
Rejoice, for through you the many-starred light now dawns,
Rejoice, for through you the many-streamed river now flows,
Rejoice, life-model of the baptismal font,
Rejoice, removal of the stain of sin,
Rejoice, laver for the cleansing of conscience,[46]
Rejoice, wine-bowl for the mixing of joy,[47]
Rejoice, fragrance of the sweetness of Christ,
Rejoice, life of mystic festival,
Rejoice, O Unmarried Bride!

## OIKOS 22

Wishing to forgive the ancient debts of all mankind,
the Creditor himself came
and dwelt among those who had departed from his grace,
and tearing up the written charge
he hears from all:[48]
Alleluia!

## OIKOS 23

We praise your Child, and likewise hymn you
as a living temple, Theotokos;
for the Lord who holds all things in his hand dwelt within
your womb,
and hallowed and glorified you,
and taught all to cry to you:

49 Only in these concluding lines does Romanos drop into the first person. He has completed a hymn to the Theotokos that is remarkable in its brilliance and concision; his strong love for her is shown by every line. But here, at the conclusion, in two brief lines he speaks personally.

Is it improper for him to call her "healing of my body" and "salvation of my soul"? Certainly, only God deserves such praise. But it's clear from the rest of this work that Romanos was not confused on that point. He repeatedly emphasizes God's initiative in salvation, and Mary's role as vessel, facilitator, "betrother." Yet here by a kind of poetic license he sums up the joy of salvation and thanks Mary for her unique role. You could call it "kissing the messenger."

May we learn from his example how to honor, and even love, this woman whom Jesus knew as mother, whom he has given to us as well.

Rejoice, tabernacle of God the Word,
Rejoice, greater Holy of Holies,
Rejoice, Ark made golden by the Spirit,
Rejoice, inexhaustible treasury of life,
Rejoice, precious diadem of godly rulers,
Rejoice, honorable boast of reverent priests,
Rejoice, unshakable tower of the Church,
Rejoice, unbreachable wall of the kingdom,
Rejoice, for through you trophies are raised up,
Rejoice, for through you enemies are cast down,
Rejoice, healing of my body,[49]
Rejoice, salvation of my soul,
Rejoice, O Unmarried Bride!

## OIKOS 24

O all-praised Mother, who bore the Word,
the Holiest of all holy ones,
as you now receive this offering, deliver from all calamity,
and rescue from impending punishment
those who cry to you:
Alleluia!

# About Paraclete Press

## Who We Are

Paraclete Press is an ecumenical publisher of books and recordings on Christian spirituality. Our publishing represents a full expression of Christian belief and practice—from Catholic to Evangelical, from Protestant to Orthodox.

Paraclete Press is the publishing arm of the Community of Jesus, an ecumenical monastic community in the Benedictine tradition. As such, we are uniquely positioned in the marketplace without connection to a large corporation and with informal relationships to many branches and denominations of faith.

We like it best when people buy our books from booksellers, our partners in successfully reaching as wide an audience as possible.

## What We Are Doing

### Books

Paraclete Press publishes books that show the richness and depth of what it means to be Christian. Although Benedictine spirituality is at the heart of all that we do, we publish books that reflect the Christian experience across many cultures, time periods, and houses of worship.

We publish books that nourish the vibrant life of the church and its people— books about spiritual practice, formation, history, ideas, and customs.

We have several different series of books within Paraclete Press, including the best-selling Living Library series of modernized classic texts; A Voice from the Monastery—giving voice to men and women monastics about what it means to live a spiritual life today; award-winning literary faith fiction; and books that explore Judaism and Islam and discover how these faiths inform Christian thought and practice.

### Recordings

From Gregorian chant to contemporary American choral works, our music recordings celebrate the richness of sacred choral music through the centuries. Paraclete is proud to distribute the recordings of the internationally acclaimed choir Gloriæ Dei Cantores, who have been praised for their "rapt and fathomless spiritual intensity" by *American Record Guide,* and the Gloriæ Dei Cantores Schola, which specializes in the study and performance of Gregorian chant. Paraclete is also the exclusive North American distributor of the recordings of the Monastic Choir of St. Peter's Abbey in Solesmes, France, long considered to be a leading authority on Gregorian chant performance.

Learn more about us at our Web site:
www.paracletepress.com,
or call us toll-free at
1-800-451-5006

## First Fruits of Prayer
A Forty-Day Journey
Through the Canon of St. Andrew

ISBN 13: 978-1-55725-469-6
234 pages
$19.95, Hardcover

*An invitation to pray as the early Christians once did.*

Join Frederica Mathewes-Green on a guided retreat through the classic Great Canon. A poetic hymn written in the eighth century, this extraordinarily beautiful work is still chanted by Eastern Christians during Lent.

## The Illumined Heart
The Ancient Christian Path
of Transformation

ISBN 13: 978-1-55725-286-9
112 pages
$13.95, Hardcover

Frederica
Mathewes-Green

Drawing on Christian writings throughout the early centuries, Frederica Mathewes-Green illuminates the ancient, transcultural faith of the early church.

## The Open Door
Entering the Sanctuary of
Icons and Prayer

ISBN 13: 978-1-55725-341-5
165 pages
$16.95, Hardcover

Frederica
Mathewes-Green

Mathewes-Green welcomes readers into an imaginary Orthodox church to view twelve of the world's most famous icons throughout the church year. Includes four-color illustrations, stories of the saints, and prayers appointed for the day.